Praise for *Crossing the Plains with Bruno*

"Annick Smith has one of the most graceful and vital relationships with time that I know of. As we see in *Crossing the Plains with Bruno*, she comes by it naturally. Her entire life—like Bruno's—has been one magical trail. I think that her grace comes from the comfort of her ability to inhabit both the past and the moment with that wonder and vitality. We in the West are lucky to have her, and this lovely, honest book."
— RICK BASS, author of *All the Land to Hold Us*

"*Crossing the Plains with Bruno* is a wise and wonderful book."
— JANISSE RAY, author of *Ecology of a Cracker Childhood*

"*Crossing the Plains with Bruno* is proof of Martín Prechtel's belief that 'the domesticated dog in particular is an ancient master of grief.' Also of joy. I knew Bruno, and I always felt when I'd see him barreling around Annick's place up the Blackfoot that the doctor was in the house. How great to find him gleefully panting and stealing our food once more as the grande dame of Montana letters resurrects a life's worth of peaks and valleys, grieves and praises our lost and living heroes, shares her emblematic personal history, and, in beneficent, lifelong, living color, herself embodies the wild beauty and endearingly offbeat culture of her tenaciously loved 'best place.'"
DAVID JAMES DUNCAN, author of *The Brothers K*

CROSSING

THE

PLAINS

WITH

BRUNO

ANNICK SMITH

TRINITY UNIVERSITY PRESS | *San Antonio*

Published by Trinity University Press
San Antonio, Texas 78212

Silhouette and cover design by Madeleine Budnick
Book design by BookMatters, Berkeley
Frontispiece: Photograph by Roy Meeks

978-1-59534-669-8 (paper)
978-1-59534-670-4 (ebook)

Billy Collins, three verses from "Dog," from *Questions about Angels*, copyright
© 1991. Reprinted with permission of the University of Pittsburgh Press.

Robert Dana, "Dog Music," © copyright Robert Dana. Reprinted with permission
of the Estate of Robert Dana.

Portions of "Dog Song," anonymous, Pima Indian, version by Joseph Duemer,
copyright © Joseph Duemer. Reprinted with the permission of Joseph Duemer.

Trinity University Press strives to produce its books using methods and materials
in an environmentally sensitive manner. We favor working with manufacturers
that practice sustainable management of all natural resources, produce paper
using recycled stock, and manage forests with the best possible practices for
people, biodiversity, and sustainability. The press is a member of the Green Press
Initiative, a nonprofit program dedicated to supporting publishers in their efforts to
reduce their impacts on endangered forests, climate change, and forest-dependent
communities.

The paper used in this publication meets the minimum requirements of the
American National Standard for Information Sciences—Permanence of Paper for
Printed Library Materials, ANSI 39.48–1992.

CIP data on file at the Library of Congress

19 18 17 16 15 | 5 4 3 2 1

For the dogs who have graced my life:

Sylvie, Shy Moon, Rasta, Betty, Little Red Dog,
and especially Bruno and Lulu

Time unseen time our continuing fiction
however we tell it eludes our dear hope and our reason.

—W. S. MERWIN

CONTENTS

PREFACE

The poet and novelist Jim Harrison has said he measures the passage of time by the dogs he has had. So do I. "The worst thing about dogs," Jim also said, "is we outlive them. . . . Hopefully not much longer." Having passed the seventy-five-year mark, both Harrison and I are ready for the moment when our pooches will outlive us. If not this batch, surely the next. And being the lost instead of the loser may be a good thing. Let them cry over us!

Writing about animals, said the poet Mark Doty in his memoir *Dog Years*, is an attempt "to bring something of the inchoate into the world of the represented." This is an impossible task. We who tell stories about the animals we love are trying to bridge the void between beings that live full lives without language as we understand it and those of us immersed in words. We know the gap cannot be bridged, and yet we are compelled to give it a try. It is like writing about love, which Doty says, "is our most common version of the unsayable."

Dogs may or may not be aware of the fragility of their humans, but we owners of pets are aware of the predictable mortality of our animal companions. Such knowing does not stop a lover of animals. Loss, we have learned, is the price of love, and love is what we are after, no matter the pain. Which brings me to Bruno, the chocolate Lab who will be a major character in this book, my traveling companion on the journey that is its core, and one of the loves of my life.

Bruno was four years old when this story began. He weighed ninety-five pounds and had functional testicles. His head was massive, his eyes yellow, and his muzzle soft and pink. Russet at the ears with fur colors deepening to chocolate brown, he was tall for a Lab and strongly muscled. Although Bruno could seem fearsome—especially when charging straight at you with his neck fur raised—he acted like a giant pup, and would remain mellower than any dog I've had, to the point of marshmallowdom. Bruno loved people, especially young women, and also Kevin, our neutered black cat, whom he tried to bugger. He was a talking dog, making moaning sounds high pitched and keening or low and guttural, which he expected you to comprehend. "Like Chewbacca," my son Alex explained. I looked blank. "The big hairy creature in *Star Wars*." Oh, the lovable monster.

I was always comforted by Brunie's warmth. He never whined. He barked only at treed grouse, bears, bulls, and intruding dogs and paid no attention to deer unless they leapt across the trail in front of him. A scavenger like all dogs, he ravaged carcasses left by hunters and munched on manure. He went nuts over grouse but, oddly for a retriever, did not like the smell of ducks. Elk interested him, though not enough for him to chase them off the meadow when they appeared at dusk in spring. Cattle were different. Bruno loved to drive them away when they grazed close to our fences. I would yell "no cows," which usually stopped him. But if a cow and calf overstepped his boundaries, he charged them, tail held straight behind and ears flopping.

Bruno believed his most serious duty was to chase coyotes. If one dared come onto our meadow hunting gophers, he took after it in a blur of speed. When the coyote reached the woods, Bruno turned back, but before coming home he had to trace the scent trail backward, zigzagging from rock pile to rock pile until he lost track.

Often, when I let Bruno out in the morning, he'd lift his leg and peer north toward Bear Creek canyon as if pointing. This was my cue. I'd lunge in his direction. He lowered his head like a fullback and avoided me easily. Then Bruno sauntered downhill past our log barn to Allen and Evelyn's place at the bottom of the canyon, where he hoped to steal the dog food they left on their porch. If their dogs started barking, Brunie would growl, but the big coward ran off when Evelyn's tiny terrier nipped at his heels. Then he continued his rounds, hoping to find a female in heat. Usually within an hour, I'd spot his thick tail swinging uphill through the tall grass. About fifty feet away he would stop and look at me, guilty but not repentant. Then, head lowered, he slunk toward the house.

Although I don't equate parents with pets, the pattern of loss is similar. To paraphrase Harrison, the worst thing about parents is most of us outlive them. Having lost my husband, Dave Smith, when I was thirty-eight and my father in my sixtieth year, I felt lucky as I turned toward seventy to have a mother nearly one hundred years old. I had not always been so grateful.

My mother, Helene Beck Deutch, came from Transylvania. She was petite, vivacious, a talented photographer, intuitive rather than rational, opinionated, hysterical in laughter as well as in anger, and in love with material things. I had no urge to follow her example, for no matter how well she manipulated her husband, all her grownup life she lived in his shadow. "I'm my father's son," I told myself. My father, Steve Deutch, was an immigrant Jew from Budapest. He took me to Cubs games and Progressive Party rallies, and discussed ideas as if I were an equal. I admired him because he was a self-made intellectual, an idealist with a Marxist bent, passionate, and intense. And he was an artist like I wanted to be.

After my father died, my mother moved to a senior residence on Chicago's North Side. She was ninety and had embarked on a new life. My sisters and I took her to places she had always wanted to visit, such as Hawaii, the Bahamas, and Los Angeles, but the only place she acknowledged as *home* was our beach house on a dune overlooking Lake Michigan near the small southwestern Michigan town of Sawyer. "It is paradise," she said in her emphatic Hungarian accent. "My paradise."

During her last years, my sisters and I took turns to visit and care for our mother, and if weather permitted, we took her to Sawyer. I usually flew from Montana to Chicago, but in May of 2003, I decided to drive. Mother was ninety-seven and still relatively vital. That journey across the plains and back to Montana is the center of this book, but circles of memory and events ripple from it—continuous—still running. The only companion I had was Bruno, the perfect pal for an aging woman returning to her mother's house.

Mom died of chronic pneumonia three years after our road trip and one day short of reaching the age of 101. We buried her ashes next to my father's in a patch of lily of the valley and red columbine on the dune overlooking Lake Michigan next to the cottage they had shared for more than half a century.

And Bruno is gone, too. Before this book was finished, his brown snout had shaded to white and his great paws were also spattered white. He was hipshot and slow to rise, a condition we shared on dark winter mornings. His backbone stood out, but his stomach was large and hard to the touch. When I took him to our vet, I insisted she examine his stomach. Only then did we discover he had a huge tumor attached to his spleen. Bruno went under the knife the next week.

The tumor was ten pounds but not malignant. The vet called to tell me Bruno was up and alert and looking around. That made me happy. A couple of hours later, my phone rang again. "Your dog's dead," said the vet.

"Dead!" I shouted. "What happened?"

"I don't know," said the vet.

"Brunie's dead," I screamed. "Dead!"

Bruno is the dog star of this story, and essential to my narrative. While driving across the vast spaces of the interior West, I often got lost in memory or flights of fancy. Bruno's presence and his needs forced me to return to the actual. He reminded me that I, too, am an animal whose existence depends on being alert to the scents and sights and hungers and emotions of the moment. Through constant company in an enclosed space, I had hoped to inch closer to understanding this dog's way of being, observing my mysterious animal as the cave people observed theirs—fascination with animals being as old as our species and the inspiration for our first and perhaps greatest expressions in art. I only partially succeeded.

I learned that dogs have memories, instincts, fears, moods, loyalties, and hatreds. They are like us in these ways. But as far as I know, dogs do not get swept up in nostalgia, speculation, or self-analysis, and, although they have hopes, they are not driven by regrets. Which is why, in a story narrated by a woman beset by the processes of aging and the imminence of death, the dog who rides shotgun is, like Sancho Panza to Don Quixote, a reminder of the physical realities outside our imaginations. He is a connoisseur of scent trails that branch sideways or backward, uphill or down, always serpentine from any straight path. I cannot know what advice Bruno would have offered if he were instructing me about how to write this book, but I like to think he would tell me to follow my nose. Life, he might say, bounds like furtive, delicious rabbits across every step of our way.

As I head toward eighty, it is easy to fall into stories about nostalgia and loss, but the world I encounter is as new and present as everyone's. In the pages that follow I have put together a mix of travel and relationships, Western history and family history, human love and animal love that centers around the two weeks I took to visit my mother. It is a chain of linked meditations, often triggered by place, about how the past impinges on the present and how that present can exist seemingly *sans* past.

Like everyone, I arrange memories, sensations, and thoughts in stories to define myself and those I love. Then I discover those stories are unstable and changing and filled with surprises, but there is consistency in them—the singular voice. I speak for myself, but as any character in my stories will tell you, I cannot see life whole or true, so experience reinvented will have to suffice. One twist of the kaleidoscope at memory's core causes the shards to fragment and re-pattern, but they are always the same shards. Now I see triangles and deep blue holes. Tomorrow there may be butterflies. That is how I believe stories work: they must be both startling and predictable, like every day's dawn.

OUTBOUND

DAY ONE, MAY 11

Mother's Day. Our recycled hewn-log house sits at four thousand feet on a meadow surrounded by forests of ponderosa pine, Douglas fir, and western larch. Above it rise the logged-over mountains of the Garnet Range, and looking down Bear Creek Canyon from our front deck, we can almost see the Big Blackfoot River. At this elevation, frost is common all spring and possible during most of the summer. With a brief growing season best suited for cabbage, lettuce, spinach, chard, snow peas, and Siberian root vegetables, I sow hardy seeds in May and wait until June to plant flowers and tomatoes. The trouble with digging my garden in May is mud. The Blackfoot Valley's clay soil clings to boots like dog shit. It tracks into the kitchen with my sons, the dog, even the cats. Mud and more mud will take a person down.

But I am not down, for May is also a time of remembrance and celebration marking my husband's death and his birthday, along with my birthday and my second son's. It is when Eric and Steve and the twins, Alex and Andrew, and their wives and children and dogs and friends come home every Mother's Day to revel in our Rocky Mountain spring—grass bursting green, frogs in the ditches, snipe spiraling down from blue skies, elk on the meadow, black bear in the thickets, and nesting bluebirds.

I love it when the family gathers, and I love it when they leave, for this is the place where I find comfort in solitude, comfort in the company of dogs. I walk with my dogs along familiar roads and into woods above our house. I look out wide windows at our meadow alive with coyotes and deer and a pair of sandhill cranes profiled on a ridge and croaking their thrilling, indescribable calls. I stand under stars in the blue-black night and imagine infinities. A friend once told me there is a Buddhist word that sounds like my name, and its meaning is "flux." I like that. "Electricity," says my longtime partner Bill Kittredge, quoting Carl Sagan, "is the way nature behaves."

May 11, my sixty-seventh birthday and Mother's Day, arrives sun swept and blooming. The meadow is speckled with magenta shooting stars and yellow dogtooth violets. I don't want to budge from my home and my family, but my mother is impatient for me to deliver her from the old people's high-rise where she lives on Chicago's North Side to our beach house in Michigan. So, to transform duty into adventure, I decide to try out the white, second-hand '98 Toyota 4Runner I have just purchased from my eldest son, Eric, for $13,000—a bargain. But I am uneasy about this new rig. SUV is a dirty word to environmentalists like me, and after thirty years of Subarus, I feel like a traitor.

"No guilt, Mom," says Steve, boyish despite his forty-five years. "SUVs are made for people like you. Not housewives in Martha Stewart land."

"Or armchair adventurers." Bill laughs his trademark laugh, low-pitched and expansive. He is a travel-book addict who loves maps and sea stories and guides to deepest Paraguay, where he ventures only in the imagination.

What I love is to head down the road into new territory and discover whatever comes to me. It has been seventeen years since I'd driven across the plains alone, and I am antsy with anticipation. No matter how much I talk about wanting to stay put, don't believe me. I am a nomad at heart. The road calls, but I want privacy, not loneliness, which is why Bruno will be my perfect traveling companion.

Bill follows my dust from Bear Creek Road to Highway 200, where he will turn west and I will turn east. It is late afternoon, a strange time to begin a cross-country trip, but I want to jump-start the voyage and get myself into road rhythm.

"Be careful," he says. I throw a kiss from my car window to Bill's, watch his Honda disappear, and take out my brand-new journal. Usually, I'm too lazy to keep a journal. I try from time to time, believing a writer should, and upon rereading am appalled by my mundane mind. But when I'm on a voyage of discovery, journaling is useful. I enter the date (5/11/03), mileage (84,561), and time of departure (4:20 p.m.). I want to keep track of where I go, spontaneously driving toward sunrise across what used to be called The Great American Desert.

Divide. Swooping down from the Continental Divide along Lewis and Clark's trail on Highway 200, I leave the evergreen forests on the west side of Rogers Pass and descend to wind-struck plains. The change in topography is startling. On the west side of the pass, the road winds steeply upward through pines and brush looking down to a sunless canyon where dark houses huddle on patches of grass. Over the top I'm struck by light and space. Rain-shadowed plains open to the horizon, and a highway taut as a stretched rubber band runs uphill and down but always straight ahead. I can see for miles and see no cars or houses, only the muted wash of spring grass, cows and coulees, buttes rising in the distance, a few horses, snow fences, weathered shacks, and the wide blue heavens above.

A. B. Guthrie Jr. christened this landscape the Big Sky in his famous book about mountain men and Indians. The name took, and as Montana license plates proclaim, this is indeed Big Sky Country. Guthrie lived some seventy miles northwest of here, where plains meet mountains near Choteau. A short ride west from his spread toward Ear Mountain is a log cabin along the Teton River that was owned by the poet Ripley Schemm, wife of the far better-known poet, Richard Hugo.

This road and that cabin take me back to a summer day in 1977. I was shooting a film with my film partner, Beth Ferris, trying to document Dick Hugo's life in a movie we'd call *Kicking the Loose Gravel Home*. The film opens with Dick driving these roller-coaster hills, heading for Ripley's cabin in his pine-green, sixties-vintage Buick convertible. The top is down. His balding head shines in the sun. He hums to a Benny Goodman tune played loud on the tape deck.

Hugo was as close as family to me and my husband, Dave. Our friendship began in Seattle around 1962, while Dave was getting a PhD in literature after giving up a career as a lawyer. Drawn by Hugo's poems about the undersides of what was then a bland middle-class city, we connected with Dick's humor and his empathy for the disenfranchised. More important, Dave and Dick shared nearly identical histories. Both had grown up poor, fatherless, and left behind by young mothers to be raised by grandparents at the margins of society. And both were self-created men of letters. Different in looks, personality, and habits of living, they recognized their brotherhood.

My connection was more female. I fell in love with Dick's voice, his warmth, his rhythms, his words. It was sexual attraction without the sex. I was an editor at the University of Washington Press at the time, a young mother trying out her wings, when an encounter with Hugo changed all of our lives. The month was July. The year, 1964. Just back from a month in Italy, Hugo sat across from my desk, where I was checking page proofs of his poems in the anthology *Five Poets of the Pacific Northwest*.

"I've quit my job at Boeing," he said. Dick's laugh was infectious. There would be no more technical writing for this poet.

"I'm going to be a Pro-fes-sor!" He rolled the syllables, relishing the word. "There's a job for an English instructor. How'd you and Dave like to join us in Missoula?"

Dave got the teaching job and I quit my editor's job and off we went that fall with Eric and Steve, our German shepherd Sylvie, her ten mongrel pups, and cartons of books piled to the slide-open roof of our green Volkswagen bus. We never looked back. Montana would become Hugo's final home, and ours, and the combination of poet and place inspired Dave and me to make our first film—*The Lady in Kicking Horse Reservoir*—a black-and-white voice-over documentary of Dick reading his poems in the places that triggered them. (He would later write a fine book about writing called *The Triggering Town*.)

Drinking heavily and abandoned by his first wife, Barbara, Dick was often morose those early years at the University of Montana, and so were his poems, and so was our film. But there was light in his darkness, for in Montana, Hugo discovered a landscape filled with forgotten towns and the forgotten people he identified with, also back-alley watering holes he liked to call home, open prairies to get lost in, and rivers filled with willing trout.

Happiness of a different kind arrived for Dick a decade later. Under his doctor's ultimatum—quit or die—Dick quit drinking. He met and married Ripley Schemm, a Montana plainswoman and poet, and through her, gained a son and a daughter, a dog, horses, a ranch-style house on Rattlesnake Creek, and Ripley's log cabin on the Teton. "I am good enough to own a home," Hugo proclaimed in "At the Cabin," a poem that celebrates his marriage. Home was no longer bars, or the loveless shack in White Center where he grew up. Home was a place he could own, like other professors and businessmen in good suits.

By 1977, Hugo had achieved national recognition and was writing and publishing as never before. "He's getting full of himself," said Bill Kittredge, who had become my lover and companion a few years after Dave died. Bill was mourning the bad-boy camaraderie he and Dick had shared during Dick's drinking days, and was wary of the limits of domestication, as well as the dangers of self-satisfaction.

"What's wrong in being happy?" I countered, knowing full well that happiness comes and happiness goes. Dick was equally aware of the pitfalls of success. His psychic homeland kept calling him back to "the old ways of defeat," as he wrote in "The Only Bar in Dixon."

Beth and I filmed Dick in his childhood home in White Center, the workingman's suburb west of Seattle where he'd imbibed those self-defeating ways, but we were more focused on his Montana successes. We could not know that a few years after we finished our film, Dick would booby-trap his own good luck by plunging back into hard-core drinking. Then, vulnerable from radiation that had gotten him through lung cancer with one good lung, he was stricken with leukemia.

When I called him for the last time in his Seattle hospital room, Dick and I chatted about the World Series that he and I were watching on TV, and he joked about the color of his skin. "You know that old jingle about a purple cow, 'I'd rather see than be one'? Well, that's me," he said. "I'm that purple cow."

Dick died on October 22, 1982, way too young (he was only fifty-nine). But at least he'd tasted that bite of contentment. Who knows what roads he might have taken if he'd survived another ten or twenty years? If he were with me this afternoon, we'd stop at the crossroads to Augusta and have a Beam ditch (Jim Beam whiskey and water) at the Bowman's Corners bar. Dave and I rarely drank in bars before we met Dick. He inducted us into honky-tonk Montana. It was a life I never fully embraced—my nature is too controlling, my responsibilities too many, and my metabolism wrong. But sitting with Hugo belly-up to workingmen's bars in Milltown or Troy or downtown Missoula, I understood why life gets wet in this dry region.

Dick rides with me now, these cascading grasslands bringing flashes of his round head and furrowed brow, the sensuous mouth set between grimace and grin, the bearlike body at rest. And his voice comes back to me, too—riveting, deep, rocketing. I open the window and recite the words of "Driving Montana," the poem that opened our film so many years ago:

> The day is a woman who loves you. Open.
> Deer drink close to the road and magpies
> Spray from your car . . .

If the poem were mine, the enamored day might be a man. Perhaps a child or dog. "No matter," Dick had said, "it's being loved . . . loving . . . that's what counts." I smile to myself, wondering if Dick had withheld a wink at those too-easy words.

No matter. This afternoon is sun gold. The Rocky Mountain Front rears sharp as a pen-and-ink drawing on the horizon west. Deer graze along the Dearborn River, and magpies *spray* from my car. The grasslands that surround me are newly risen and, yes, Dick, "Open." I want to shout to the wind, to the sun, "Goodbye, life-as-usual, I'm truckin'!"

Sun River. Bruno and I continue northeast on Highway 200, looking out to buttes and benches of a classic western landscape, descending imperceptibly toward the Sun River Valley. Beyond Fort Shaw (built in 1867 to protect settlers from the Blackfeet Indians whose lands the settlers had invaded) the land turns green, irrigated from the Sun River Irrigation Project. The Sun is a short river. It rises practically within eyesight on the east side of the Continental Divide in the Bob Marshall Wilderness near the massive limestone escarpment called the Chinese Wall. The river's sun-splashed waters fall through elk preserves and picture-perfect dude ranches to this bottomland of hayfields and wheat farms.

The highway runs through the small town of Sun River and is its main drag. On both sides are tree-lined streets and modest bungalows whose backyards and sheds and chicken coops are scattered along the flood-prone bottoms. I decide to take Bruno for his first walk. We park beside the bridge that spans the river, and Bruno leaps out of the car. Red-winged blackbirds flush out of willows as we stir the tall grass. The Sun is high with run-off and Bruno looks at me, hesitant in this strange territory, but he is game for any walk, every river, and so am I.

"My sweet boy," I whisper, wrapping my arms around his wide, furry neck. I inhale his musky scent. He's got no demands that conflict with mine.

I taught school in this isolated town for a week in the early eighties, commuting twenty miles each morning from Great Falls because there was no motel here or anywhere nearby. Those days (and for most of the next forty years) I worked freelance on scripts, essays, and stories, trying to support my kids any way I could, short of taking an actual job.

"Why not get a job?" is a refrain I've heard over and over from Bill, from my kids, even from friends. But jobs are anathema to an old back-to-the-earth hippie like me. Jobs will tie you down, and I prefer to be free, even if that means being poor. While the boys were in school, I wrote grants and ran summer writing workshops and was director of a literary center in Missoula called Hellgate Writers. And I hired on for weeklong gigs as a Filmmaker in the Schools for the Montana Arts Council, teaching children in prairie towns and on Indian reservations.

In Sun River I taught filmmaking to seventh- and eighth-graders, and we made a claymation film. I remember the slimy worms of clay; the ranch kids with rough, red fingers piling one worm on top of another; their delight at seeing a creature morph and grow as the Super 8 film sped through a projector. (This was before camcorders.)

Fetching water for Bruno's dish, I step into mud that is black and squishy like that long-ago clay. It clings to my sandals and between my toes. I place the water under Bruno's muzzle. He looks away. I splash some drops on his nose, trying to tempt him. I know he is thirsty, but the crazy dog won't drink.

Jessy's Gift. Bruno was a gift from my granddaughter Jessy. I'd been partial to German shepherds and did not fancy Labrador retrievers, but I wanted Bruno—and only Bruno— because he would tie me closer to Jessy, my longed-for first grandchild, whom I had only recently come to know.

Jessy had been born without my knowledge when Alex and Jessy's mother, Robin, were eighteen. They'd had a weeklong affair the summer after high school but were not in love. When Alex came home for Christmas from his freshman year at Berkeley, he went to a sports bar with a couple of buddies. Robin was sitting at a table with some friends, and when she stood to greet Alex, he saw she was pregnant.

"Who's the lucky dad?" asked Alex.

"You, you idiot!"

The timing was right, but Alex wasn't positive. He went back to Berkeley without telling anyone except his twin brother, Andrew, that he might become a father.

Robin had been the wild child of her devout Catholic family, but she was determined to keep her baby even though it meant staying home, growing up fast, and not escaping to the San Francisco Bay area college she'd dreamed of attending. Alex simply could not deal with the responsibilities of having a child, especially since he wasn't sure it was his. So after Jessy was born in April 1987, it didn't take much urging from Robin's lawyer father to convince him to relinquish all claims to the baby. And when

Robin got married two years later, her husband adopted Jessy with no challenges from Alex.

Ten years passed and Alex was home again for Christmas, this time from graduate school at the University of Texas. "Let's take a walk," he said. "I have something to tell you." He looked so somber my heart plummeted. It crossed my mind he might have AIDS, which was epidemic among sexually active young folk. As we climbed the icy logging road through the forest, Alex remained silent.

"Okay," I said, "you gotta tell me what's wrong."

"Nothing's wrong," said Alex. "But I've been keeping a secret." I waited for his next words. "What I mean is . . . I'm a father. I have a daughter ten years old."

"A daughter!" I was dumbfounded. "Thank God! A child is good!" I hugged him, and then the fury rose. "Ten years! How could you keep me in the dark? I'm your mother."

"At first I wasn't sure," he said, "but Max and Spencer have kept up with Robin, and they say Jessy Rose—that's her name—is pretty and smart and funny, and I guess there's no doubt who her father is . . . she looks just like me."

We stopped on a ridge, looking down at the red metal roof of our log barn, and I peered up at my tall, dark-haired son, newly aware of the distance between us. "If I'd told you sooner, there's no way you'd have stayed away," he said, putting his arm around my shoulder. "I wasn't ready for that!"

Alex was right. Had I known his secret, I would have done most anything to be with my first grandchild. I calmed down, glad that at last he was taking steps toward making contact. The fact that Robin and her husband had divorced made the job easier. Still, it would take two years and an encounter with Robin at a mutual friend's funeral before Alex and Jessy found each other.

"She wants to do it," Robin reported to Alex. "She wants to meet you. I've always told her who her father was. She's known since she was a little girl."

At their first rendezvous, Robin, Jessy, and Alex ate steaks in a back-country bar and café on an elk preserve near Seeley Lake. Over red wine and a Roy Rogers, they studied the baby albums Robin had brought, showing Alex what he had missed. Robin memorialized the meeting in a snapshot that sits on my bedroom dresser. Jessy's bangs fall over her forehead. She wears a long, flowered skirt and stands a head shorter than Alex, but their resemblance is unmistakable. Wearing a blue shirt and cowboy boots, Alex holds his arm stiffly around his daughter's shoulder and smiles a self-conscious but infatuated smile. "She has a good appetite, and she's funny," Alex told me afterward. "I really like her."

A couple of weeks later Alex and Robin brought Jessy to the ranch. At twelve, her dark hair fell to her shoulders. She was an A student and tall, with large brown eyes and a cupid's bow mouth. I couldn't take my eyes off her hands. Jessy has an athlete's hands—large, with long narrow fingers—and not only her hands but her gestures are duplicates of Alex's, which are replicas of Dave Smith's. I never imagined that gestures could be as genetic as eye color or hair, passed down in this case over three generations. And I wondered if the emotions that engender gesture can also be inherited. Or the personalities that give rise to those emotions.

For me and for Jessy it was love at first sight. We had no baggage, no guilt, and no history to overcome. And the connection we made was cemented by the gift she gave me on her thirteenth birthday. Jessy had stayed up all of Easter night to midwife her black Lab, Tucker. In the otherwise all-black litter, two chocolate males claimed my attention—a feisty, pointy-nosed guy, and a plump placid fellow with classic features.

"Take the big one," Jessy said. "You won't regret it."

I did. And I don't. We named him Bruno, and when he was six weeks old, I came with Steve to fetch him from the double-wide trailer near the logging town of Lincoln where Robin and Jessy lived on her family's compound. On our way home, Bruno slept the seventy mountainous miles from the headwaters of the Black-foot River to our log house on Bear Creek Road. When I set him in front of our kitchen porch, our mature German shepherd mix Betty walked diffidently toward the newcomer. She did not growl as she usually did when strange dogs came to visit, but gave Bruno a sniff upside his ears and under his tail. Satisfied, she trotted off toward the more compelling barbecue grill on our back deck where steaks trailed tantalizing odors and someone might toss her a piece of gristle or fat.

Bill Kittredge had brought the steaks. A self-exiled rancher from the high deserts of eastern Oregon, Bill is a big man who likes thick rib eyes marbled with fat. Steve broiled the steaks on the gas grill. He had been laid off from his job and was studying public policy in graduate school. With thick, close-cut brown hair, an ingenuous smile, and an incipient beer belly, Steve looks younger than his age. He was, and still is, our hunter, gatherer, and gourmet cook.

At our round wooden table, we passed Bruno from lap to lap. I let him lick my greasy hands, kissed and petted him. When he fell asleep, I set him on Betty's bed. Stars came out and we ate and drank until spring's frosty night drove us indoors. I went to gather up the puppy and carry him to my bedroom, but he was gone. Gone! The meadows and forests outside our lit-up deck were black in the moonless night. My stomach turned cartwheels. I had left my baby dog alone where coyotes howl, and great horned owls hunt small mammals, and cougars lurk at the edge of the cliff.

"Where's Bruno?" I asked Betty. "Go get him!"

Betty looked up at me, wagged her tail, and tried to lick my hand. Useless. Steve and Bill and I searched the deck, the garden, and the dark spaces behind the house by the compost heap. We checked the foundations where a puppy might bed along sun-warmed cement. No Bruno.

I called and called, "here, puppy, here" and "come, Bruno," doubting if he knew his name, or knew me well enough to respond. And I was struck with fear. Unless it is a lost child, there is little as heartbreaking as a lost puppy or kitten or knob-kneed foal. What drives the pain wrenching the heart, the electric shock to the brain, is the anticipated death of innocence.

Bill, who is no dog nut like me, stumbled around calling and whistling. Steve searched the woodshed. He dropped to his knees, shining his flashlight around stacks of split wood. "Found him!" Bruno had curled up on a pile of sawdust. In months to come I would learn that he hankers for den-like hideouts. Bruno naps on cool ground under our porch, beds on the couch in the small, dim, book-lined room where we watch TV, and runs willingly to his pen and doghouse. Our bewildered pup, perhaps searching for his mother and littermates, had nested in the first den he came to, oblivious to our cries and safe within its enclosure.

Follow Your Nose. Highway 200 ends a few miles east of Sun River at Vaughn in a T-junction with I-15. I turn east on the freeway, driving twelve miles to the Great Falls city exit. Then I get lost. I find the bus depot in the city's center. "Last bus's gone," says the burly man in a gray uniform. I don't want a bus, just directions on how to get to Lewistown.

My plan when I entered Great Falls was to drive north to Fort Benton and watch the Missouri swirl around the huge circular cutbank where the river bends toward town. From there I could follow its course along the famous Lewis and Clark water route, losing sight of it as it winds east toward Pompey's white pillars. Then I'd head for the Hi-Line near the Canadian border and run straight east on Highway 2. But that route is out of my way and would eat too much of my limited time, so I ask the bus man to direct me to a more direct road across the plains. He points me toward Highway 87 going southeast and I feel like a dummy.

This is a road I know well, but I was in such a hurry to leave home, I neglected to bring along a map—any map. Seemed more *flaneur*-ish to follow my nose, Bruno fashion.

Nose—I get stuck on that word. It causes a shudder of free association. *Nose*, the word not the thing, reminds me of Pinky McNamara, Dave Smith's best high school buddy. Pinky lives in Minneapolis and is suffering from early-onset Alzheimer's, disappearing in body as well as mind. It is hard for me to imagine pugnacious Pinky—Pinky the football player, brilliant businessman, and self-made millionaire—growing repetitive and dim, shorn of his trademark wit. He was white-haired when I last saw him, but lean as the racquetball champ he used to be. He will die before I finish this book, and I'm glad I will not witness his transformation. Call me coward, but it is hard to see friends disappear. That is the second worst thing about growing old. The first worst is your own disintegration.

I met Dave Smith when I was sixteen going on seventeen, and Pinky shortly after. The two had grown up in Hastings, a small town on the Mississippi River south of St. Paul, Minnesota. Both came from the wrong side of the tracks. Pinky's father was alcoholic and had abandoned his wife and five sons. Dave was illegitimate, his father a married Swedish farmer who seduced his sixteen-year-old mother, Virtue. After Dave was born, Virtue had what was called a nervous breakdown (the first instance of schizophrenia that would rule the rest of her life) and went off to Chicago to study at a Bible college, leaving Dave to live in poverty with his grandmother and six aunts.

Pinky and Dave became local heroes in Hastings when their basketball team won the state championship in 1951. They were ambitious and smart young men, determined, as Dave would say, "to get the hell out of Dodge." Their road out was paved with athletic scholarships. When I began dating Dave he was on a basketball ride at the University of Chicago, and Pinky played Big Ten football for the Minnesota Gophers. Dave was fair-haired with a perfect Nordic nose, while Pinky and I were well-endowed—his snout was Irish potato, mine, prominent Jewish. My mother was constantly after me to get a nose job. "You can look like Elizabeth Taylor," she said. I laughed at her. I did not have violet eyes, big breasts, or a twenty-inch waistline. "Leave me alone," I said.

Mom would convince my sister to have the operation, and Kathy would become a model, a dancer, an aspiring actress, and, eventually, a filmmaker—also Pinky's sometimes and longtime lover. I, however, was adamant to stay as nature intended. I never dyed my prematurely gray hair, never even pierced my ears. Nowadays when I look in the mirror I'm not so sure I took the right path. "I should have an eye job," I complain to my sisters, try Botox, maybe a face-lift.

"If you had a nose full of nickels," Pinky teased me long ago, "you'd be rich." Pinky had the nose for gold. His schnoz was biggest. He was the only one of us who got rich—rich enough to become a member of the University of Minnesota's Board of Regents, donating eleven million dollars to the school that led him from poverty to wealth and whose alumni center bears his name.

Mothering. Past Stanford, Montana, we enter the Judith Basin, a territory bounded by the Judith River, the Little Belt Mountains, and the old cowboy town of Utica, where the artist Charlie Russell learned to ride and drink and draw. I pull off at a rest stop where the historical marker says that here, at the turn of the nineteenth century, for the first time in Montana, agriculture replaced mining as the primary economic activity. In 1910, three trains loaded with homesteaders passed through Judith Gap every day. Abandoned shacks across the plains are testimony to pioneer dreams gone south. I, too, am an immigrant come west and have an abiding interest in pioneer stories—especially the stories of women—which has led me to many creative projects, including the making of my first feature film, *Heartland*, shot not far from here in Judith Gap country. But I'm not thinking about pioneer women right now, I'm thinking about my failures as a mother.

I walk Bruno among cottonwoods near a fence bordering a hayfield, keeping as far as I can from the highway. He follows squirrel scents and is happy in his sniffing. His pleasure makes me happy, too. I believe I am more solicitous about this dog's comfort than I was about my children's. That recognition turns me sad and guilty. Especially when my son Andrew reads my manuscript and nods in agreement.

"Yeah," he says. "You're right about that!"

Andrew is a tender, thoughtful parent to his two little girls— more child-centered than Dave and I ever were. But he is over forty and a tenured professor, and he and his wife, Courtney—a creative director for advertising clients—make a decent double income. Unlike me in my mothering days, not only are they capable of middle-class security, but they deliberately chose to have children in midlife.

Dave Smith and I had married in 1955, when I was nineteen and he, twenty-two. Early marriage was common those days, along with chancy birth-control methods. Within a year we had a son; a year and a half later, a second son. When the unplanned twins were born in England ten years later, we were still young, but kids no longer. We were in England because Dave was on sabbatical from his English professor job at the University of Montana. If we'd known I was carrying twins, we might have had second thoughts, but I'd refused to be X-rayed and my doctor could hear only one heartbeat, so off we went.

By my eighth month I was huge-bellied and almost unable to walk. I told anyone who noticed, "Maybe I'm carrying an elephant." The boys were delivered full term in a red-brick hospital in Amersham in Buckinghamshire, at the expense of Britain's universal health care system. Andrew—six pounds—had been squinched up under my ribs, and his heartbeat melded with mine. Alex—eight pounds—lounged comfortably at the low end of my uterus. My cinnamon-skinned West Indian midwives were large and gentle and spoke with a musical lilt. "You pop them out easy as two peas in a pod," said one. "They beautiful boys," said the other.

I was one depleted thirty-one-year-old mom, stick-thin and exhausted, with hair turning gray and teeth decomposing. My doctor, Mr. Butcher, instructed me to not even try nursing my brood if I wanted to keep all of us healthy. I admit I was relieved. The prospect of nursing two babies with money running out and a move to Spain in the works was intimidating. Yet I felt proud to have produced such bounty. "I've mothered a litter," I told Dave, identifying with female bears or dogs rather than the pale British mums in the maternity ward.

At thirty-four, Dave was suffering from high cholesterol, fatigue, shortness of breath, and pains in his arm, which turned out to be angina. Dave knew something was drastically wrong, but his Missoula doctor had advised him only to stop drinking milkshakes and quit playing basketball. We would not know until he was hospitalized with a mild heart attack just after we returned from Europe that Dave had inherited a metabolic disease that clogged his arteries with undigested fatty deposits. Although he volunteered at the University of Washington Medical School on research for anti-cholesterol drugs, the research was in an early stage and did not help him. And since surgeons there had ruled out a bypass operation, Dave could do nothing but eat carefully and walk and wait. The disease would kill him six years later.

"I was your age and just starting on my own," I remind Andrew. But economic survival was not all I was after. When Dave died, I was thirty-eight. The twins were finishing first grade. Eric had graduated from high school and would soon be adventuring in South America. Steve was a wild and crazy kid but doing fine in high school. And I was looking at my hole card.

All my life, like many women raised in the fifties, I'd followed my man, taking any job to help support the family. With Dave gone, sad as the circumstances were, I was free to take my own road. My new career began when I agreed to produce a series about Northwest Indians for Spokane public television. The job had first been offered to Dave, exactly the job he was looking for. He was to be producer, and me the associate. Ironically, the phone call arrived two months after his death.

"Sorry," I said to the station director, "you're too late."

He was silent a moment, then replied, "How about you?"

No way, I thought. He insisted. The job meant a regular pay-check, a start in a new profession, and a way to bury my grief in work. But raw as I was, and with low self-esteem, I was certain I'd be fired within a year. Which is why I left my kids in Montana under the care of friends, commuting the two hundred miles to and from Spokane every weekend. I believed it was best not to uproot my boys any more than they'd already been uprooted—at least until I proved myself.

After a long and extensive search, I hired an Indian director, writer, and crew (very hard to find those days) and began working on the series with seven tribes and an advisory board that included leaders from Spokane's urban Indian community. The realities of working with Indian people and tribal cultures whose complexities, rivalries, and deep connections I could not begin to understand almost drove me—the idealistic, romantic, Jewish wannabe Indian from Chicago—to despair.

The job stretched into two years. It stretched me beyond my limits, but I held on and was able to bring the twins to Spokane for a year. And although the nine-part *Real People* series did not get aired nationally on PBS, it would be shown on regional public television all over the West and is now available on You-Tube. During its production, I traveled to meetings in Washington D.C., Seattle, and New York and met younger media women who'd been nurtured by the feminist movement. They encouraged me to keep on making films that mattered. Which was the only thing I wanted to do. But nothing comes without a price, and the price for my career as a producer was paid, in part, by my kids.

"So, yes," I say to Andrew when he remarks on this part of my manuscript, "I wasn't the best mom. I sure could have been better. And I'm really sorry I didn't give you all the attention you deserved."

As I walk the edge of the highway, Bruno pulling at his leash, I realize how much my life has changed. I'm no longer a film-maker but a semi-retired part-time writer. My house is paid off. I get Social Security and Medicare. Bill takes me to exotic places, helps me remodel my house, and buys me fancy restaurant dinners. With few obligations and time on my hands, I relish the opportunity to care for Andrew's daughters, Tilly and Elodie. I take them to Vietnamese noodle lunches, let them help me mash potatoes and strain applesauce for Sunday dinners at the ranch, treat them to ice cream cones every Friday, even shop with them at Target. And this leads me to wonder if only grandparents are sane and selfless enough to care well for our offspring's offspring.

Charlie Russell Country. I load Bruno into my rig and, with no cars in sight, make a U-turn across Highway 87 to get a good photo angle on the sunset that is lighting up these plains. I know the photos will not be good enough even for postcards, but the horizontal perspective, the geometry of buttes, the dominant sky in stained-glass reds and oranges and purples are Charlie Russell pure.

This is the cowboy West that Russell ran off to in 1880 when he was sixteen. America's fantasy was enacted those days in horseback work tied to land and weather, and in the romance of Indians. Young Russell cowboyed on ranches in Judith Gap country, lived with the Blood (Blackfeet) Indians for a year, and recorded the life he witnessed and the past he imagined in pen and ink, chalk, and oil paint. I don't see what Charlie saw, but what I see is worth recording. Horse herds and cowhands are rare these days, most Indians wear cowboy hats and live on reservations, and there's new wealth to be gleaned from the skies in wind generators that tower over grasslands near Judith Gap like giant storks feeding on the constant, swirling winds.

The real pots of gold, however, rest under the thin soil of the northern plains in a fracking bonanza for oil and gas just east of here, and in huge deposits of coal being strip-mined on reservations and ranchlands to the south. Mining in Montana is booming again, but there is still land in the Judith Basin for millionaire ranch hobbyists, retirees wanting escape from urban stress, and ranchers who keep holding on. This landscape of buttes and gullies and grasses glittering scarlet and purple and gold in the setting sun remains intact. Like Charlie, it is packed with jokes and violence. Intractable. Inebriated.

It is getting dark. I'm hungry. I enter Lewistown, pass up the Motel 8 (can't stand the plastic-clad beds), and drive the main street, happy to see red-brick storefronts as they were a century ago. We stop at the Yogo Inn, named for Yogo sapphires pried out of the Judith Basin's bedrock. I order a last-minute Yogo burger while checking in, for the restaurant closes at nine. A slim-hipped fellow in jeans and cowboy hat saunters in after me—a local. The blonde waitress flirts at his booth. They chat and laugh. He gets his burger first.

I sneak Bruno in the motel's back door. Have to kick him in the butt to get him up to the second floor. The mutt is phobic about stairs with open slats; phobic about cliff edges. How did I get such a chicken dog? We reach the top, and I realize our room is on the ground floor. Now I have to get Bruno down the stairs.

He braces his feet and won't budge. I nearly choke him with the choke chain until gravity does its work.

Finally, we settle into our room. I turn on the TV. Bruno looks up at me and, without permission, jumps on my bed. I don't feel like watching crime dramas tonight. I leaf through the *Dog Music* anthology I've brought along and find one that fits my mood, if not Bruno's. He cocks his head as I read it aloud:

Dog
BILLY COLLINS

I can hear him out in the kitchen
his lapping the night's only music,
head bowed over the waterbowl
like an illustration in a book for boys. [. . .]

Then he makes three circles around himself,
flattening his ancient memory of tall grass
before dropping his weight with a sigh on the floor.

This is the spot where he will spend the night,
his ears listening for the syllable of his name,
his tongue hidden in his long mouth
like a strange naked hermit in a cave.

OUTBOUND

DAY TWO, MAY 12

Prairie Morning. Before heading east out of Lewistown on Highway 87, I walk Bruno along the railroad tracks for a couple of blocks. The air is cool and the grass along the verge is dewy. We skirt a fenced canal and scare up a few mallards. Bruno prances like a horse, big head up, eyes alert, taking in dozens of new scents. He veers toward some tufts of bunchgrass. Unlike many dogs I have known, Bruno never defecates on a lawn or, God forbid, a sidewalk or street. This is not because I taught him to behave. He is a self-civilized chocolate Lab.

I stop for gas and have to fight my sense of outrage. It costs twenty-four dollars to fill this car's tank. (A few years later, the cost will be four dollars a gallon.) My old Subaru got about thirty-two miles per gallon; this rig, about twenty. Maybe I was stupid to give the Subaru to my kids. I fill my mug with weak coffee. Call Bill on the cell phone. His voice has a wistful, almost petulant edge. "I miss you," he says. I don't miss anyone. It is 8:30 and I chide myself for getting a late start. What do you mean by late, I ask myself? As Bill would say, "It's not a footrace."

I'm driving the center of Montana. Land flattens in rolling plains broken by coulees. Some are cracks in the earth's skin, some are great gullies; and as they erode from high plains down toward the Missouri River's gorge, they become deeper and wider, like side canyons of the Grand Canyon, branching every which way from the Missouri's main channel. Laced with cottonwoods and choked with brush, these are the famous Missouri Breaks.

Today they hide rabbits, deer, and cougars, but in the 1880s the breaks were thick with horse thieves. Vigilantes who called themselves The Stranglers took severe retribution. Most were landed men, respectable for that reason only, and their leader was Granville Stuart, a book-loving rancher who would become the state's first librarian and a chronicler of Montana's history. Those righteous men of property hunted the riffraff like they hunted wolves. Dave Smith was so taken by this story that he wrote a movie treatment called *The Stranglers*. Later Tom McGuane and Jim Harrison collaborated on a screenplay about the same vigilantes. A bastardized version of their script was made into the movie *Missouri Breaks*, starring Jack Nicholson and Marlon Brando, in which Brando stole the show and lost the story.

In real life, about thirty suspected horse thieves were tracked down and lynched by the vigilantes, some in front of their wives and kids. The thought makes me shudder. This cold and violent country seems haunted by cold and violent men. I cannot help thinking of West Texas and George Bush, or Dick Cheney from the high plains of Wyoming, both avowed Christians posing as cowmen and shamelessly advocating torture and greed in the service of power.

On this high plain the sky is dominant, merciless, and prophetic. Weather arrives wind-borne from the horizon some fifty miles distant, and you can see it coming. Winds from the south and west bring moisture or warm chinooks; winds from the north and east carry cold and drought. Only the wind is constant. It buffets the 4Runner and, when I open the door, nearly knocks me to my knees. Coming at me are purple thunderfists cracked by lightning. Rain in black lines laces the clouds to earth. The storm roars past, and soon we are driving under wisps of cumulus strung by the jet stream. Sheep clouds play peek-a-boo with the sun. Here are the wide-spreading blues and luscious green hills that George Catlin painted more than two centuries ago. But where are the clotted herds of bison?

The last wild bison on these plains were nearly hunted out before the hordes of settlers finished them off, taking aim from train windows at the decimated herds, piling bison bones into white towers. But the land remains well grazed. In many places it is overgrazed. Big ranchers, bankers, and corporations consolidated the properties of failed homesteaders. Their black white-faced Hereford/Angus cattle speckle the range. Few humans are needed to tend the lands of big agriculture, which is why the nearly deserted cow towns Bruno and I pass through are weathered like fence posts. Grass Range. Teigen. Winnett. Going, going . . . soon gone.

Heartland. The next creek will be Box Elder. It is high like the Musselshell, which runs through Harlowton about fifty miles southwest of here. Harlowton was where my dream of making a fiction film came true. With good friends Connie Poten and Claire Beckham, Beth Ferris and I formed a nonprofit company in Missoula called Wilderness Women Productions and spent two years developing our project.

Filmed in 1979, *Heartland* was the first theatrical movie to reflect the revisionist school of history about women in the West. It depicts the realities of love and work, life and death on a homestead ranch. With the support and advice of Wallace Stegner and A. B. Guthrie Jr., as well as the technical and artistic know-how of director Richard Pearce and co-producer Mike Hausman, Beth and I—two unknown and largely untried Montana filmmakers—were able to get funding from the National Endowment for the Humanities in Washington D.C. not only for research and development but for our film's production. I believe we have the distinction of being the first and last feature to be financed in this way.

Heartland was a new breed you might call "feminist western." It was based on the true story of Wyoming widow Elinore Stewart, who in 1910 became housekeeper for a curmudgeonly rancher, homesteaded the land next to his, married him for practical more than romantic reasons, lived through devastating winters and the death of a baby son, and survived to write about her experiences in a book called *Letters of a Woman Homesteader.*

Beth wrote the script, which was revised by Bill Kittredge. The film starred Rip Torn, Conchata Ferrell, and a Missoula child actress, Megan Folsom. We headquartered in Harlowton with a crew from New York, Hollywood, and Montana during the ice-cold spring of 1979. I'd been afraid Mike Hausman—a New Yorker who was one of the most sought-after line producers in the business—would alienate the railroaders and ranchers in Harlowton, but I was wrong. Mike packed his pockets with twenty-dollar bills. He wore jeans and an army captain's cap and sported a revolver on his hip. Driving his rented pickup from hardware store to dry goods store, to cafés and gas stations and motels, he bought building materials and hired locals to construct our sets and work in production. Before he was done, most of the tradespeople in Harlowton were wearing white metal buttons adorned by a heart and the words I LOVE NEW YORK.

By our wrap party at the end of May, a good many locals as well as ranchers and cowboys from Judith Gap, Garneil, Martinsdale, and Two Dot had worked on or in the film. They drove and branded cattle for our roundup scenes, served meals to cast and crew in the root cellar of our log-house set, and danced at the filmed wedding of Elinore and Clyde, with the mayor of Harlowton playing the role of preacher.

I will never forget that railroad town or my room in the fading Victorian-style Graves Hotel. Because I was executive producer,

I had dibs on one of the third-floor tower bedrooms. Rip Torn preferred to live in a trailer with his rifle, roping regalia, fishing rod, and a fifth of Jim Beam. And Conchata Farrell had chosen to take rooms with her two Siamese cats in a more modern motel. But the Graves, with its homespun bar and restaurant, was our center of gravity. During rare moments of rest I would look down from my room's tall bay windows at budding cottonwoods along the river, or across the railroad tracks to the roundhouse where locomotives huffed and shuttled. It was good to be reminded that the town's life did not revolve around our here-today-gone-tomorrow, low-budget film.

The movie chronicles a year in the lives of Elinore and Clyde, but our shooting schedule had to simulate four seasons in eight weeks. We needed snow for winter and sun to fake summer. Local forecasters had promised us a spring snowstorm and our blizzard arrived in April, later than we'd hoped and two feet deep. Then we waited for the snow to melt, waited for green up in the foothills of the mile-high Snowy Mountains, which did not occur until mid-May, when filming was almost finished. Only then could we shoot the cattle drive and branding scenes; see cowboys running cows on green grass; focus on a bouquet of shooting stars, yellow bells, and lupine held out by Elinore's daughter Jerrine to her hopeful, long-suffering mother.

Today, the Graves has been shut down and stands like a disheveled widow above the railroad yard, which is also deserted. But the town is alive with alternative energy. North of Harlow, where we filmed cows and abandoned shacks, a forest of gigantic wind turbines rises above the naked prairies, creating electricity from the constant winds. And up-country out of Garneil, across from the ranch where we shot *Heartland*, Mike Hausman bought eight hundred acres, married our production secretary, Pam, built a ranch house, had a son named Colt, hauled in a caboose for a guest dwelling, and nurtures a herd of Montana bison, some so tame they will eat from your hand.

Prairies Preserved. At Mosby, I cross the Musselshell. It is one of my favorite rivers, passing through wetlands thick with waterfowl and between limestone walls tinted a lemony yellow or the buff color of doves. Rock cut from the river's canyons provided building blocks for the banks, courthouses, schools, and jails in the towns along its reaches, giving them a warm glow and the illusion of permanence. The buildings have outlived the nineteenth century's railroad-centered, small-town culture that created them. But those towns, although crumbling, are still alive.

I love the word *Musselshell.* It flows from tongues as it flows through Ryegate, where Bill and I caroused one summer after an artists' gathering in Barber. Our friend Ted Waddell, who grew up on a local ranch and has become a well-known painter of abstract cows and horses, took us to the annual "testicle festival" at the Ryegate Bar. We sampled fried Rocky Mountain oysters (bull calves' testicles), washing the leathery nuggets down with Beam ditches (bourbon and water—*ditchwater* in the vernacular). Bill, who grew up on a ranch in eastern Oregon, pushed his greasy paper plate away. "These are awful," he said. "You should've tasted 'em done right. Throw the nuts in hot coals and fish them out with a stick. Crunchy outside, tender inside."

The Musselshell courses east from Ryegate past the rough, coal-mining country around Roundup where United Mine Workers were organized and buried their dead in an elaborate, wrought-iron gated cemetery, and where union leader Tony Boyle was born. From there the river turns north from Melstone and empties into the Fort Peck Reservoir and Charles M. Russell National Wildlife Refuge. This is where the American Prairie Foundation, in partnership with the World Wildlife Fund, is conserving and restoring a patchwork of public and private lands that, in their best dream, would encompass more than three million acres, extending from Malta in the northeast to Lewistown at the southwest corner, and would include in cooperative management the existing Charles M. Russell Federal Wildlife Refuge (1.1 million acres) and the Missouri River Breaks National Monument (700,000 acres) as well as the Nature Conservancy's Matador Ranch and bordering portions of tribal lands.

The preserve already harbors mammals, fish, and wildfowl that were resident when Lewis and Clark came through in 1804. A birdwatcher like me can spot larks, hummingbirds, chickadees, flycatchers, goatsuckers, herons, kingfishers, owls, sage grouse, wild swans, hawks, eagles, and more. When I toured the preserve with a naturalist guide a couple of years ago, we saw threatened prairie dogs in prairie-dog towns and a small population of endangered black-footed ferrets that prey on them. Deer, antelopes, black bears, coyotes, and elk find shelter in rough breaks and wetlands, while a herd of genetically pure bison grazes on restored native grasses. Eventually, I hope, these prairies will once again offer protection to wolves, grizzlies, wildcats, and eagles—the native predators that ranchers nearly wiped out generations ago.

"It will be like the Serengeti," says one supporter. "Only bigger."

Wrong, I think, not the Serengeti. A team of scientists from Cornell University thinks otherwise. They've suggested that the environment of the prehistoric Great Plains, which was shaped by extinct mega-fauna such as wooly mammoths and saber-toothed tigers, could be re-created by transplanting elephants and lions from Africa and Asia. I imagine the response of a lean old cowboy to herds of elephants on his range. Lions. Camels running wild. His legs are bowed from a lifetime of riding horses. His stained old Stetson is pulled low over skin pitted and tough as his saddle. He lets go a stream of snus. The notion of turning the prairies into some Wild West exotic species zoo is what he expects from city people. "Bullshit!"

It is a bitter irony that hardscrabble ranchers like him are being displaced by "environmentalists" (a pejorative term in these parts), just as their homesteading ancestors displaced the Indians. And it's ironic that their herds of cattle are being replaced by bison. I wonder how many locals will refuse to sell to the Prairie Preserve conservationists, forgoing economic security to defend the cowboy culture that gives them identity, if not wealth. Some will sell their land and help manage the preserve. Others will move to Arizona or Florida or Billings. Still others have found that choice so repellent that it helped drive them into hate groups such as armed militias and the Aryan Nations.

Aryan Nations is a place I don't want my mind to go right now. Driving alone has lulled me into a semi-trance, and I am as weary of dire reflections as I am of pipe dreams. So I put a poetry CD in the deck, not knowing what I'll hear because there is no label or cover that tells me. The scratchy, old-man's voice with a lilt is unmistakable:

> I will arise and go now and go to Innisfree,
> And a small cabin build there, of clay and wattles made:
> Nine bean-rows will I have there, a hive for the honey-bee,
> And live alone in the bee-loud glade.

Yeats reciting "The Lake Isle of Innisfree." I know these words by heart because I memorized them at New Trier High in 1950s Winnetka. I was a stranger there—Hungarian Jewish city girl wearing mother-made dresses amid the blue-eyed Christian suburbanites with their cashmere sweaters. But the Midwest is not my home anymore. Me? I live in Montana in my bee-loud glade.

Ranch Road, Brown Ranch. I turn off the poetry, roll down my window, breathe ozone and pollen and wind. Here is the prairie vibrant with morning. Bruno wants out even more than I do. He shifts about in his car-pen. Somewhere past Sand Springs I spot a dirt road into a ranch called Brown's. There are no buildings or ranch hands in view and no signs warning that trespassers will be shot on sight. I drive up the track a few hundred yards and open the tailgate. Bruno jumps to the ground. He leaps and pirouettes, then stands on his back legs, paws on my chest to give me a thank-you lick. Who says dogs don't have emotions?

We walk along a coulee. Meadowlarks on fence posts serenade each other and us. Their song is yellow and bright, like their breast feathers. We scare up three whitetail deer. They bounce high through the sagebrush, hooves up in perfect synchronicity, tails waving like flags, and I laugh because they are funny. Bruno gives them a look but does not take chase. He would chase a rabbit, go nuts over a sage grouse, run off a coyote, and challenge a bear. But deer are not of interest to him except as meat.

Prickly pear cactus is spiny underfoot, and I rub my fingers through knee-high silver sage to gather its perfume. Bruno heads straight into the stream that cuts through the coulee. He swims snout up in circles, making grunts of delight.

"You're a pig. A big fat piggy." He smiles his dog smile, "happy as a clam in butter," as Ray Carver used to say.

I could amble through this prairie with Bruno for hours. But no. Mother enters my thoughts for the first time since I left Bear Creek. I wish I hadn't promised her I'd be in Chicago so soon. Maybe I'll call and tell her I'll be a couple of days late. I try to push her image from my mind—a tiny old woman at the bay window of her thirty-second-floor apartment peering wistfully at the Chicago skyline and waiting for me. Another image. She is sitting on her rose-color sofa in her off-white living room, dozing next to the telephone. She is waiting for a phone call from me. Waiting for her eldest daughter to walk into her doorway.

That daughter wants nothing more than to immerse herself in grass, sage, and sun. To feel no urgency. To think of no future. But duty calls. The 4Runner glares white in the distance. I've got to quit daydreaming. We have only begun today's long ride. I turn to retrace my steps. Bruno lags behind, as reluctant as I am to leave the actual prairie and return to the abstract highway. I have to whistle him back. Before climbing into the driver's seat, I pick a pungent stalk of sage to hang over the rearview mirror. Its perfume lasts for days. I will take this prairie with me.

Jordan. We drive into Jordan, a prairie town clustered like a herd of sheep among engulfing grasslands—population 364 and dwindling. I am struck by a sense of isolation as tangible as the scattered trailers in weedy lots, the shacks and painted bungalows with their pickups and snowmobiles. Dusty shade trees and wind-blown garden plots are poignant in their impermanence, while the paved main street sports a false-front bar, a café, a few stores, and a Ford dealership. From its edges, the town tumbles onto arid plains with no other settlement in sight. Fifty miles to the next gas, the next store.

Jordan is the only real town in Garfield County, which is the size of Connecticut (4,491 square miles) and carries a population of about 1,500. This adds up to a density of about 0.35 persons per square mile. In the booming 1920s the county's 5,000 inhabitants occupied 1,530 homestead farms averaging 571 acres. Recently, there were fewer than 300 farms or ranches, each averaging 6,947 acres. Not enough land for a cattle or sheep rancher to make a decent living.

Hate grows like thistles in the cracked soil of such despair. Jordan, for example, is where, in 1996, armed men and women who called themselves the Freemen defied the sheriff in a standoff lasting eighty-one days, refusing to pay taxes. They declared themselves a separate government and shone in media lights until the FBI dispersed them and police jailed the leaders. But I have only good memories in Jordan. This is where Bill's car broke down on a long-ago road trip, and where the motel proprietor asked if we were paleontologists. (The area is famous for its dinosaur digs.) Yes, we nodded. Paleontologists for sure.

While waiting for a new fuel pump to arrive from Billings, we borrowed a Ford pickup from the car dealer and drove north to Fort Peck to visit its mammoth earth-filled dam—a Works Progress Administration project made famous by Dorothea Lange's photo on the cover of *Life* magazine's first issue in 1936. We did not find prehistoric bones around the many-fingered reservoir, but we did see a hardhat tree. It sat in front of a prefab cabin on the false lake's rocky shores—an old juniper hung with safety helmets colored yellow, red, fluorescent orange, blue—artifacts of the tribe of construction workers whose Riviera this is. In the slanted light of dusk the hardhats glowed like strange fruit against a landscape that looked to my unschooled eyes as barren as the moon.

Jordan is the town where Greg Hemingway (youngest son of Ernest) came to doctor at the doctorless clinic, driving about two hundred miles from Bozeman each week. When he was caught dressed in drag at the Hell Roaring Bar (I imagine a flounced red dress and high heels), he fled home. But the town wanted him. They ran an ad in the *Bozeman Chronicle:* "Come back, Dr. Hemingway." He ignored their plea. "We didn't care what he wore," said the nurse at the clinic. "We needed a doctor. Ask anyone."

Greg was a talented writer, and his slim book, *Papa,* is an exposé of the tragic effects of fame on the father and on the son. Greg came to live with his own son, a student at the University of Montana, in Missoula in the early eighties. In those days Missoula was a haven for hard-drinking, partying, mostly macho writers, and Bill tried to help Greg out of legendary jams such as appearing in hot pants and heels in the ladies' locker room of the Missoula Athletic Club. But nothing could stop his self-destructive rampage. I met him near the end of his Missoula days, expecting an exotic character, and was surprised to encounter a small, gray-bearded nondescript fellow. This was at a literary event at the university, where Greg was heckling a respected elderly woman poet, shouting, "Your time's up! I came to hear Bill Kittredge."

Poor Greg's heart gave out in a Miami jail. He had undergone a sex-change operation in middle age and taken the name Gloria. The newspaper reported that Gloria had been picked up on the median strip of a Miami freeway wearing only high heels and panties. Indigent at his death, and as powerless as the street people who shared his cell, the youngest child of Ernest Hemingway left an estate of $5.3 million for his children and ex-wife to fight over. When I read that news, I could not help thinking that Greg/Gloria should have stayed in Jordan, where extinct beasts and misfits are tolerated as long as they offer something of value.

Makoshika. East of Jordan the road rises sharply and dips up and down for miles. This is mining country, rough and rocky. I return to my poetry CD. W. H. Auden is declaiming. A wild turkey ambles across the highway. In front of me a pickup pulling a horse trailer stops on the steep grade to let the turkey pass. I'm not sure why this seems significant. Maybe listening to poetry makes everything seem significant. We begin the long haul across noon-bleached plains through Circle to Glendive.

Bruno moves restlessly from his bed behind me. He bumps against the passenger seat and angles toward the rear. I throw him a dog biscuit. He settles down on the hard mat under the open back window and looks back at me with baleful yellow eyes. I feel guilty. I throw him a second biscuit and return to my poetry. Here is the voice of Wallace Stevens; no way to mistake Gertrude Stein. Bruno sighs. I am sure he is thirsty as well as hot and bored, but I don't stop. "Stay tough." I speak to Bruno as if he were one of my boys. "Pull up your socks."

Just south of Glendive, in the badlands above the Yellowstone River, there is a secret little paradise I remember from twenty years ago. I was working for peanuts as Filmmaker in the Schools for the Montana Arts Council, and my most distant gig was Glendive High School. For two weeks I instructed the media class of that eastern Montana agricultural, river, and railroad town (population about 4,900). My students were children of druggists, hardware store owners, salesmen, ranchers, teachers, laborers—a cross section of white, rural, western America—and the movie they wanted to make was, of course, a western.

With much prompting, the kids wrote, directed, acted, and shot the film in one week. We had to use the art council's Super 8 cameras—an inferior technology—but were lucky in having the badlands of Makoshika Park as a location. Real horses were *verboten* for liability reasons, so we used stick ponies made by the teenagers or borrowed from their little brothers and sisters. I can still see those kids in Levi's and cowboy hats hopping on their stick steeds through knee-high bunchgrass. They hoot with laughter, chase each other with toy rifles into a clearing filled with blue lupine, red paintbrush, wild geraniums. We lose track of any narrative beyond hilarity.

Returning today, I pull into a scenic turnout. Bruno trots ahead, and it's good that no rangers are near, for he is not on a leash. We walk out into a fantasy of cones and pillars, buttes and mounds striated in earthy colors: sienna, apricot, and gray. It's not surprising that dinosaur fossils have been found here—triceratops and the much smaller thescelosaurus, dating back more than sixty-five million years—for these badlands include a strata of the famous Hell Creek Formation that also runs through the digs north of Jordan.

Bruno charges nose-down through a grassy draw thick with lupine and yellow balsamroot. We amble into a pine grove where bluebirds call, and climb an outcrop topped by giant sandstone mushrooms that have been carved by eons of wind and wind-driven rain and snow. I look down at the blue glitter of the Yellowstone River snaking east across the plains. Chickenhearted

Bruno stays well back from the precipice. He is digging frantically at gopher holes. Our ramble has consumed more than an hour and I am tempted to nap in the shade of a sulfur-yellow rock, but the sun is sinking. "Back to car-jail," I yell. "Let's go!"

East of Glendive, we enter I-94, our first freeway of this trip, but only for twenty-eight miles. We turn south onto Highway 7 at Wibaux, a historic old town and the county seat, which dates back to the 1870s, when Texas cowboys drove their cattle through it on their way north after the Civil War. Wibaux became a thriving shipping center where ranchers such as Teddy Roosevelt came to sell their cows, and then it declined. The oil boom of the 1970s brought a brief revival, which was highlighted by an all-day street brawl that is legendary in these parts; and if I could look forward ten years to 2013, I would be shocked to see Wibaux and the other almost-ghost towns in this Montana/North Dakota borderland booming again. This time, the energy extravaganza will be the fracking frenzy of the Bakken oil sands deposits. From Canada south across the plains, there will be huge trailer parks, man-camps, fast-food joints, new roads, new bars, full jails, and full employment. But this afternoon, the tree-shaded streets are empty. Commerce lies elsewhere.

Highway 7 parallels the North Dakota state line and the Little Missouri National Grasslands, and I'm glad to be back on a two-lane surrounded by hayfields. Shadows lengthen. Daylight turns amber. I gird myself for hundreds of miles of night driving and am tempted to stop at the next motel. But I know I will not. Across the plains in Chicago, my mother is counting the hours. A woman coming up on one hundred knows every hour is precious. I speed toward Baker, then turn east on Highway 12 into Teddy Roosevelt's Wild West.

New Country, Old Country. On a bluff above the highway, a mammoth cut-steel cowboy on a bucking bronc welcomes me to North Dakota. This southeast corner of the state is a place of badlands, broken treaties, cattle ranches, and replanted bison. In a few years it will be booming from the fracking horror show, but for now it is a forgotten country on a road I've never taken.

We cross the Little Missouri at Marmarth and pass through lignite coulees and bentonite bluffs that roll past Fort Dilts, a fort so insignificant I can discover nothing about its history. At Bowman I gas up, find a free map of North Dakota (my first map since leaving the ranch), and try to place myself. The road I'd like to take forks north toward wild grasslands and herds of hunched bison. If I turned off on Highway 85, I could hike up White Butte, which, at 3,506 feet, is the highest point in North Dakota. I look back at Brunie. He raises his big head. "That fact alone," I tell him, "is all I need to know about this state." (Just kidding.)

Bruno responds with a nasal, guttural noise somewhere between a snort and a moan. He seems to be asking, Mom, why are we sitting in this car and going nowhere? A pickup's door slams at the pump behind me. A child cries. I fasten my seatbelt and drive east on Highway 12 past Scranton, Gascoyne, Bucyrus, Hettinger— tree-starved burgs tidier than Montana's cow towns. I wonder if Bucyrus refers to Greece or Persia, but I am on the wrong track. Bucyrus (population 23) was named in 1908 after a steam shovel manufactured in Bucyrus, Ohio. The machine arrived by rail, along with the town's inhabitants. Painted yellow, its stack rose above the railroad station and post office—the most vivid object for miles.

Stony, arid, short-grass plains encircle me. Once, this place was touted as the Promised Land. Women in babushkas descended from third-class railroad cars along with their bushy-bearded men. They came from Germany, Sweden, Norway, Wales, Poland, and Russia. I put myself in their sabots and imagine bewilderment. This was not the land pictured in railroad brochures, with pumpkins three feet high and heavy bunches of grapes. This land was poor, but it was free. Free land to Europe's disenfranchised was worth the taking, even if it meant risking life, culture, and soul.

To survive in such places as this North Dakota hinterland demanded toughness hard for us soft-handed descendants to imagine. Examine portraits of Great Plains homesteaders in historical museums, and you will see faces of stoicism. Worn families, stern and formal, stand outside sod houses displaying a piano, a pair of oxen, a set of china, a hand-cranked washing machine. Such treasures, along with languages of their homelands and stories the old people told, were what they carried from the past to plant in the beaten grass of the American steppe.

When I think about North Dakota, which I rarely do except when I'm in it, my mind turns to immigrants because I, myself, am first-generation: Hungarian Jew by family origin, born in Paris, emigrating to Chicago before I could talk, then moving to Seattle at twenty with my first baby and husband, finally roosting for nearly forty years in a river valley in western Montana.

My mother's people came from towns astride the Hungarian plains—a richer earth than the Dakotas but a herding, horseback culture as well. Under the Hapsburg Empire and until the 1930s, Jews had lived there in relative peace among Catholic Magyars and Calvinist Transylvanians. Wealthy Jews owned large estates, were respected artists and intellectuals, and consorted with their gentile counterparts. Bourgeois Jews like my grandfather Pollack on my mother's side—a blue-eyed, red-bearded orthodox religious leader—could own a store in town and live on a farm.

My mother's mother, Serene Pollack Beck, told us stories about growing up on the southern *puszta* along the flood-prone Tisza River in Senta—a small city marked by turn-of-the-century art nouveau architecture, parks with formal gardens, and a quay along the wide, cottonwood-shaded river where the entire town could promenade. Senta was Hungarian before World War I, but the city and its fertile floodplain farmlands were given to Serbia after the 1918 Austro-Hungarian defeat. A remnant Hungarian population remains, but the Jews are long gone—victims of the

Holocaust or survivors fled to places more welcoming. Some of my grandma's closest relatives were among those who stayed.

"It was terrible," Grandma Beck told us girls, gathered around her armchair on the back porch of our Chicago apartment. Tears fell from her red-rimmed, faded brown eyes. (My grandma wept often and easily—she wept at any sad memory.) "They killed my brother in his house. And Ilka, too."

In the story, as I recall it, a cocky Nazi soldier amuses himself by harassing Grandma's older brother, Ignatz (nicknamed, ironically, Natzi). Ignatz was a religious leader in the community. He lived in the country house where Grandma grew up with her eleven siblings.

"Our house was white," she said in her broken English interspersed with Hungarian phrases and French words. "We had geraniums . . . *rouge* . . . how do you say it?"

"Red," we chorus.

"Yes, red geraniums in the windows. And paprika [pronounced POP-ree-ka] in big bunches hanging on the walls."

Grandma closes her eyes. She tells us her brother had a long red beard like his father's. (In the sepia-toned picture of him in our family album, the beard seems gray, and he wears a skullcap.) I imagine the German soldier (or more likely a soldier from the fascist Hungarian militia) strutting into the courtyard. He thinks it is funny to pull the Jew's beard. He laughs. Ignatz struggles to get away. His daughter Ilka screams. She grabs the soldier's arm, trying to stop him from hurting her father. I'm not sure if this drama is totally imagined or if it stems from Grandma's tale. The ending, however, is fact. Ignatz and Ilka were shot dead in their home by a fascist soldier.

Black Cherries. Driving toward dusk through this almost-empty landscape, I keep thinking about my Hungarian family and about the road trip I took with my sisters a few years ago, tracing our

heritage through Hungary and Transylvania and the corner of
Serbia along the Tisza that I think of as Grandma's Land. That
trip was in the month of May, as this trip is, but the resemblance
stops there. The lush countryside we passed through was splashed
with villages and farmsteads and surrounded by fields whose rows
of leafy plants we struggled to identify. Could they be potatoes?
No. Squash? No. Beans? Finally, I got it.

"Paprika!" I shouted. Here were fields of peppers—red, green,
and yellow peppers. The Hungarian vegetable supreme.

We arrived in Senta on a warm Sunday afternoon. The town
square, with its gardens and fountains, pathways and green
lawns, was filled with roses in bloom and families dressed in
party clothes drinking beer and champagne. Many were dancing to folk tunes and gypsy songs played by a small Hungarian
band—grandfathers and young couples and children dancing the
czardas, my mother's favorite dance. The occasion was a wedding.
Actually, two weddings: the formal Serbian wedding being held
in the Grand Hotel's ballroom; the Hungarian one, outdoors in
the square.

Kathy, Carole, and I stood at the park's edge outside the Grand
Hotel's café in our jeans and capris and sandals, tapping our feet
and taking pictures. We were obviously American, the only tourists around, and—inevitably—a portly Hungarian gentlemen
offered us free beers and invited us to dance. Which, of course,
we did, twirling and stomping while disapproving matrons with
hennaed hair (all three of us are white-headed) looked at us
askance.

Afterward, in a celebratory mood, we went to the city's historical museum, hoping someone there could lead us to the Jewish
cemetery where, we were sure, our Grandma Beck's relatives were
buried. The stout attendant shrugged when we asked her in our
halting Hungarian. We repeated our question in English and she
shrugged again, deliberately ignoring us and our question.

Since we'd already paid our entrance fees, we went into the main exhibit rooms and studied relics of ancient cave people who once inhabited these river bottoms. There were also bones of extinct aurochs and mammoths. And embroidered costumes from peasant cultures of my grandmother's time. Then we noticed two college-age girls studying an exhibit about Anne Frank in an adjacent hall.

"Do you speak English?" I asked the slim, dark-haired girl who, from her looks, might be Jewish.

"Yes," she said. "Can I help you?"

As luck would have it, the girl had recently returned from a year as an exchange student in Seattle, and, better than giving us directions, she and her honey-blonde friend were eager to lead us to the walled Jewish cemetery at the edge of town.

The cemetery stood on a sloping hillside looking down on railroad tracks and hayfields sprinkled with blue and yellow wildflowers. It had a wire gate and a monument with a six-pointed star dedicated to victims of the Holocaust. Our new friend explained that the grounds had been recently mowed for a commemorative ceremony, and, although she was not Jewish, she'd played the clarinet during a musical interlude. Surprisingly, she saw no Jews there—either local or from out of town. "I think they're all gone," she said.

The girls trailed along with me and my sisters through a sloping forest of weathered, tumbledown, limestone gravestones dating back a century or more, but none recent. Some were stacked nearly on top of each other, others tipped precariously toward the ground, and many were lettered in fading Hebrew. Looking for stones with my grandma's surname—Pollack—we located a dozen or more, for it had been a large family, but we found none with the first names of my great-grandmother or great-grandfather. At least none we could recognize.

Clasping the wire gate shut behind us, Kathy, Carole, and I

embraced the sympathetic girls, took snapshots, and picked ripe black cherries from small trees bordering the cemetery. The sweet yet bitter taste of those cherries is what I take back from that ancestral burying ground. It is the taste of my grandmother's home, my mother's childhood, and my inheritance.

The Brothers Deutch. I grow sore eyed and butt weary driving and driving away from the sun. Bruno shifts in his car jail, moans to let me know he's still part of this deal, and nuzzles the back of my neck with his wet nose. I dip into his bag of treats and toss a Milk-Bone over my shoulder. "Sorry, boy," I say. "Hold your horses. Miles to go before we rest." He grunts and retreats to his bed while I return to obsessive speculations about the transformative journeys of my parents.

My mother at eighteen had fled Romanian-occupied Transylvania with her widowed mother to join her biologist brother in Paris. My father, also in his teens and with no schooling beyond the eighth grade, left his family in Budapest to try his luck as a sculptor in Paris. Like many immigrants, they were determined to reinvent themselves. And though the histories they fled were often tragic and violent and perhaps best forgotten, by leaving that past behind, my mother and father did not realize they were leaving their offspring bereft of historical identity.

They were not the first of my family to emigrate. By 1920, a few of my father's mother's relatives had sailed to the United States. Although some put roots down in Cleveland, the largest branch chose Chicago. Don't ask me why Chicago. Maybe the prairie city seemed more welcoming than New York's ghettos for people of the Hungarian plains. Maybe they knew friends in Chicago's Hungarian Jewish colony. Probably it was serendipitous—one family member following another until a clan had assembled.

The first I know of were Matyas Braun (a brother of my grandmother Deutch) and his wife, Anna. Matyas and Anna opened a grocery store and lunch counter on Chicago's West Side and invited my father's oldest brother, Alfred, to work in the store and live with them. So, in 1921, at age nineteen, Alfred arrived in Chicago. He was a talented illustrator, having quit commercial school to become an artist, and he brought along his portfolio: humorous semi-abstract posters advertising cigarettes or night-clubs, brightly colored patterns in art nouveau styles, life draw-ings from an art class. Clerking in his uncle's store would be his first step to becoming American. He quickly learned English and began to look for work as a graphic artist.

Alfred was fair skinned with sandy hair and a receding chin. He stood over six feet tall—a gangly and aloof young man who might pass for gentile. He appears in old photos sporting a felt hat, dressed in tweed knickers or three-piece suits, and, in one picture, wearing a tuxedo—a dandy. But although his sardonic sense of humor was obvious in his illustrations and cartoons, his face in every photograph is unsmiling.

Alfred achieved a level of success by selling whimsical cover art and drawings to *Chicago Magazine* but was rejected by the *New Yorker*, where he might have established a national reputation. My sisters and I know little about his life except that he worked for a lighting manufacturer and designed decorative Craftsman-style lamps for Chicago's new opera house—intricate objets d'art, which still hang in its hallways. But when the economy crashed after October 1929, such luxurious creations crashed with it, and so did his prospects.

Examining the oversized portfolio of Alfred's drawings and posters that my father lovingly preserved, I notice he signed his artwork "Dutch" rather than "Deutsch," and this was also the name on his business cards. Here was a man who wanted no part of being Jewish or Hungarian. I can identify with that. Growing up during and after World War II, I knew that if my parents had stayed in Hungary, there would be no them and no me. Being a Jew was dangerous, even in the United States.

The danger struck home when I was ten. My mother had

taken me shopping in the labyrinth of Marshall Fields' bargain basement. Daydreaming and bored, I wandered down dark aisles until I was lost. Trying to retrace my steps, I was accosted under the escalator by an unkempt bearded man in khakis: "Come here, you nice little Jew girl." He tried to grab my skirt. Reached for my thick, black pigtails, saying "I won't hurt you." His breath was foul. I jerked away from his touch. Ran as fast as I could go. Only later did I wonder how he knew I was a Jew. Would he have come after me if my hair were blonde and my nose turned up?

By age twelve, I was fed up with having odd first and last names that were hard to pronounce and set me apart—apartness being what adolescents fear most. I decided to change my first name to Annie, since Annick is a diminutive of Anne in the Celtic language of Brittany, where my parents had honeymooned and where their favorite chambermaid was called Annick. Then, by eliminating the letter *e* from Deutch (which my family had already changed from the original *Deutsch* during World War II, for obvious reasons), I could change my last name to Dutch. I telephoned the Cook County courthouse to inquire about how to legally become Annie Dutch, but the red tape was too cumbersome and I was wary of betraying my mother and father by choosing a name that had not originated with them.

While Alfred struggled with his new identity and looked for artistic recognition in Chicago, my father and his middle brother, Eugene, shared a walk-up above a whorehouse in Montmartre for a few months in 1927. Gene signed on as an apprentice in Brancusi's workshop, and the forms he studied there would mark his later work as a ceramic artist. My father carved away at his wooden sculptures, reminiscent of Rodin/Henry Moore but more diminutive. Since neither could survive on his art, Gene hired out as a carpenter, and my father made false antiques in a workshop on the Rue Mouffetard.

My father loved Paris. And so did my mother. They met in

gatherings of young Hungarian émigrés, romanced each other, got married in Paris, became French citizens, and had a French child—me. Paris, they thought, would be their home forever. But Gene was restless. In 1927–28 he followed Alfred to Chicago and joined his uncle Matyas's household. Short and dark, carefree and handsome in a John Garfield way, Gene was something of a playboy.

"I'm sure he had an affair with his aunt Anna," Mom told me one afternoon as we studied photos in a family album. "How do you know?" I asked. "See. Look there. Your grandma cut Anna's face out of the pictures. Why else would she do that?"

In 1929 Alfred went back to Hungary to visit his parents. Family gossip and snapshots of Alfred on a Lake Michigan beach with a fair-haired girl in a cloche suggest he had a gentile girlfriend. The story I remember is that my grandparents would not accept a wife who was not Jewish. Another version is that the girl was Catholic and *her* parents would not allow the lovers to marry. Kathy is convinced the girlfriend story is a ruse. Alfred, she believes, was a closeted gay and suffered his secret in despair. No matter what the cause, we know that Alfred was in a dark state of mind. In a scrawled postcard from Budapest to my father in Paris, he wrote, "Your Honor . . . a broken . . . poor, talent-less, without hope . . . your brother Alfred."

A few months later, Alfred went to Paris to see my father Pictures taken by my mother show the brothers gallivanting, waving hats, playing tennis, having fun. But the high times were short-lived. Alfred returned to Chicago in 1930 as the Great Depression took hold, and his life remained stalled. His mind dipped into its own depression. He sent my father another picture postcard. In it, Alfred stands behind a counter in his uncle's store wearing a long white apron. It reads, "I am selling candy, cigarettes, and sodas, but I have ambitions. . . . Life is not amusant!"

Soon afterward he and Gene rented a dingy apartment on

Chicago's West Side, where, in March 1931, at age twenty-nine, Alfred committed suicide. I believe he'd been contemplating self-destruction for a while, although no one caught his message. My clue is photographic. The last image we have of Alfred is a close-up portrait of him sitting in an armchair in his uncle's house. The words below the image read, "Remember me." Why else would a young man say such a thing in a photo he sent abroad to his favorite brother?

Only Gene could have known the triggering cause behind Alfred's suicide because he lived with him and was closest to him. And Gene knew the method, for he discovered his brother's body. At the inquest he testified that Alfred's death was caused by "temporary insanity brought on by ill health." We have only the vaguest notions of what he meant by "ill health," for there is scant mention in letters or gossip that Alfred was ill, and Gene never spoke about this traumatic event to me or to my sisters, or even to his daughters. And my father, who was devastated by his brother's death and bore the grief all his life, also remained mute, pretending ignorance when asked.

Our mother was the only elder who would talk to me and to my sisters about Alfred's suicide. "It is impossible to know why he did it," she said when we quizzed her. "I don't even know—I stopped asking—you couldn't ask, because Gene fainted if anyone questioned him too closely."

"I think it was gas," she surmised, and she was mostly right. From copies of his death certificate that Carole recently discovered, we know that Alfred died from inhaling "illuminating" fluid. Maybe he brought the fluid home from his job at the lighting company. Maybe it was kerosene, but no matter which method he chose, his dying must have been painful and horrible.

Alfred died in the midst of the Depression. He was likely clinically depressed. But not alone in desperation. Suicide was common during the Depression, and even more common among recent immigrants from central Europe. In *The Captive Mind*, the Polish poet Czesław Miłosz believed estrangement was at the root: "People decided to leave their villages and little towns, as a man considers suicide. They weighed everything, then went off into the unknown, but once there, they were seized by a despair unlike anything they had ever experienced in the old country."

My grandma and grandpa Deutch would never know the cause of their eldest son's death, for Gene and my father and the Chicago relatives told them that Alfred had died of pneumonia. Protection by deception was a tradition in my family—a practice common at the time, but paternalistic and condescending and, in my opinion, a way to play God. Still, I have to admit that deception in this case was a sensitive way for children to show love to elderly parents already bereft and brokenhearted.

My grieving grandparents sailed to Chicago in 1931 to mourn Alfred and to commiserate with Gene. After returning home to Hungary they must have felt more abandoned than they did before they departed. By 1935 they were ready to start new lives. Paris was a possibility, but they had no ties to Paris beyond my father. Chicago was better. Alfred was buried in Chicago, and Gene lived there, as well as Matyas and Anna. So, in January 1936, with Hitler rising in Germany and no children or grandchildren or future in Hungary, my father's parents left their homeland and history and immigrated to the United States, where they moved into an apartment with Gene and his dog Teddy on Chicago's Near North Side. This was where, about a year later, my parents, with baby me in their arms, would join them.

All Flesh Is Grass. I motor without stopping to relieve Bruno or my aching backside along Highway 12 across flat, semi-arid ranch-lands, always east and a bit south, and my mind stays busy with thoughts of immigrants. I know very well about Jews in big cities but had never heard of Jewish pioneers in North Dakota until

I read some of their stories in Sophie Trupin's memoir, *Dakota Diaspora: Memoirs of a Jewish Homesteader.*

Sophie's family, along with other Jews from Russia and Poland, homesteaded just north of Bismarck in the small town of Wing during the early 1900s. They were part of the second wave of homestead migration sponsored by transcontinental railroads. Wagon-train settlers had come west during and after the Civil War, when the Homestead Act of 1862 promised free land to citizens and intended citizens—160 acres if the claimants lived on and worked the land for five years. The fertile tallgrass prairies of the Midwest were quickly settled, but the arid western plains remained empty. Since the railroads owned huge sections of the plains, they needed a steady influx of settlers, passengers, and commercial goods to make profits. Railroad propaganda touted the riches to be found in rough country like these badlands, and poor folk in Europe as well as from the slums and ghettos of American cities stepped out of third-class passenger cars, sure that rain would follow the plow.

The western plains had been part of the hunting grounds of horseback tribes such as the Kiowa and the Sioux, but after the Indians had been subdued and confined, and after the bison herds had been killed off, reservations were opened to white settlers under the allotment acts of 1909. The revised Homestead Acts promised larger units than the original 160-acre parcels, which were adequate in Ohio but hopeless on the plains, yet the increased acreage was not enough to support a family. Many quit farming and, like Sophie's parents, moved to towns that mushroomed along spur lines. Other failed farmers went off to cities where they could survive. Those who stayed formed a society more agrarian than cowpoke. Their tidy settlements have little resemblance to the helter-skelter outposts of fur hunters, gold diggers, Texas cowboys, prostitutes, and ne'er-do-wells who bedded a while farther west.

We skirt the Standing Rock Reservation and ease into South Dakota at Lemmon. This is a region made familiar by the writer and poet Kathleen Norris, whose *Dakota: A Spiritual Geography* is one of the western texts I most admire. Norris grew up in Hawaii but, after a career as a poet in New York, moved with her poet husband, David Dwyer, to her grandparents' ranch near Lemmon. She ran that ranch for twenty-five years. Norris reversed the pattern of literary mavens such as Willa Cather and Mari Sandoz, who fled from confining homes in open spaces to freedom in New York among a community of intellectuals and artists. They never went home to live, except in memory or art.

I took the Norris route, fleeing my city upbringing to root in the West's thin earth. Open spaces and wild nature have become my home, my inspiration, and my delight. But Kathleen's journey was spiritual in a more conventional sense, leading her to live in a monastery as well as a ranch house. The monastery offered solace of a kind I will never know, but I believe I share a kinship with Norris in the solace of the plains—this ancient seabed gone to grass.

"All flesh is grass," Norris writes, quoting the Bible, "and it has real meaning for people who grow grass, cut it, bale it, and go out every day in winter to feed it to cows." The Dakotans she describes with sympathy but no sentimentality know the beef they eat is the flesh of grass, and the corn and grains they eat are also grasses. Any way we cut it, we are creatures of grass, quickly risen and easily mowed.

When I die, I can imagine being buried on some plain like this one or on my smaller patch of meadow, or I might want my ashes scattered in the obliging wind. My flesh would be transformed into grass, or better, into buttercups, shooting stars, lupine, and the cupped lavender pasque flowers (state flower of South Dakota), whose stamens are yellow with pollen and whose silky stalks rise from snow at Easter. Imagining such glory, I recall the whole line from Psalm 90: "All flesh is grass and its beauty is as the flower of the field."

Sitting Bull. If I were to turn south on Highway 63 out of McLaughlin, I could wander deep into the Standing Rock Reservation, home of the Hunkpapa band of the Teton Sioux. The road would lead me to Sitting Bull's camp, where the warrior, hero, holy man, and leader lived his last years in a log cabin. But I do not go there, for I have read that the camp is located at the bottom of a nearly inaccessible gully along the Grand River, not far from where the chief was born in 1831.

By the fall of 1890, Sitting Bull's camp had become a center for Ghost Dancers on the Sioux reservation. They danced for days, danced to exhaustion, and fell into trances. The dancers believed if they continued long enough they could dance a new world into existence, where dead Indians would be resurrected, bison returned to earth, and white invaders destroyed. This was not an ancient religion from the tribe's prehistoric past but a religion only one year old, which began in 1889, when a Piute named Wavoca had a vision during an eclipse of the sun.

Wavoca's Ghost Dance religion swept into the camps of desperate tribes, bringing hope to the hungry and dispossessed when all hope seemed lost. It made white authorities such as Indian agent Major James McLaughlin fearful, for it attracted angry young men such as those in Sitting Bull's camp who believed their muslin dancing shirts marked with magical symbols would render them bulletproof. Agent McLaughlin telegraphed Washington D.C. for advice and directions, and the commissioner of Indian Affairs replied with orders to arrest the "leaders of excitement or fomenters of disturbance."

The first Indian policemen McLaughlin ordered to arrest Sitting Bull resigned en masse. So he appointed new police under a Yankton Sioux named Bullhead. Backed by about one hundred U.S. cavalry armed with a Gatling gun, forty-three Indian police invaded Sitting Bull's camp before dawn on December 15, 1890. Three men dragged the chief from his bed and tried to pull him onto his horse. One of Sitting Bull's defenders shot Bullhead, and Bullhead's gun went off, shooting Sitting Bull in the head. He took seven bullets in the ensuing panic and died.

It tells us something about our culture that a town on a major U.S. highway is named after the no-account agent McLaughlin, while there is no good road to Sitting Bull's camp; and even if there were, a visitor would find no remnants of the chief. His log house was dismantled and hauled to the Chicago World's Fair of 1893 and likely ended in a garbage dump.

"Indians!" Sitting Bull had shouted the August before his death, as he battled to prevent Congress from legislating a land-grab division of the huge Sioux reservation, "there are no Indians left but me!"

We pass quickly through Mobridge, an Indian/tourist town with a big bridge spanning the Missouri. Bruno is restless and hungry and thirsty, but I find no good place to offer him relief. Once, the Missouri River was the main passage west for traders, explorers, soldiers, and settlers, but it's been dammed and tamed by the Army Corps of Engineers, and its artificial levels are a matter of legal contention between commercial interests who want enough water for barges to run downstream to St. Louis and environmental groups who want more uneven natural flows to save breeding grounds for endangered plover and sturgeon.

I decide not to stop at Sitting Bull's monument on the Missouri's bluffs and hurry on with Bruno in mind, finding no resting place until we pull in at a picnic grounds and pond east of Mobridge. Bruno gives me a look, either resentful or grateful, and streaks off along a short trail at water's edge. I follow as fast as I can. Finally, he is a happy dog. His rear end cants from side to side. His thick brown tail wags in slow but constant motion. Bruno wades into the pond, takes a short swim, finds a stick along the bank, and drops it at my feet. I throw the stick and he retrieves it. Water is his element, and he enjoys it as much as the water birds who, having noticed him, are paddling toward the center of the pond: white pelicans, egrets, Canada geese, mallards, and red-tufted mergansers dipping tail-up to feed on the marshy bottoms.

As Bruno and I play fetch-the-stick, Indian families arrive in pickups and vans. I watch fathers and mothers fish with children, their long poles casting lures into waters streaked rose by the setting sun. I feel like the stranger I am, having invaded their sacred ground, but the scene enthralls me and I stay a discreet distance away until the sun disappears. Now is the moment cinematographers prize—the "magic hour" just after sundown when light drenches all it touches in gilt and silver. The world, for a brief time, loses its shadows. This is Sitting Bull's inheritance.

Aberdeen. We reach Aberdeen at 8:30 p.m. Mountain Time (9:30 Central). The town is flat, flat, flat—so flat the city's engineers had trouble designing a drainage system for its tree-lined streets. Residents think of Aberdeen as an oasis, but it's no oasis for me. The commercial strip announces modest prosperity, which cannot be gainsaid on these lonely prairies, but box stores are no sop for the beauty-hungry eye.

I check into the Comfort Inn and leave a thirty-dollar deposit as dog insurance. I walk Bruno on the grass patch behind the motel with my eye on a Quizno's across the rail fence, watching sadly as the café's lights go out. I can't find an open sit-down restaurant, but Wendy's is serving. I order southwest chicken salad and a baked potato to go. Then I stop at the liquor store for a Heineken to take back to our room. I flop on the bed too tired to read a dog poem or turn on the TV. Behind my closed eyes a red highway bucks and roars.

Next morning over bacon and eggs, I will open Linda Has-
selstrom's *Roadside History of South Dakota* and discover that this
watering hole of twenty-five thousand souls was founded in 1822
as an outpost for Scottish fur traders. By the 1880s, Aberdeen
had become a major railroad crossroads inhabited by Scandina-
vian farmers. That year, three hundred Welsh bachelors stomped
out of third-class coaches and took up homestead claims. Three
hundred bachelors! I imagine Swedish husbands sighing in relief
when the Welshmen had earned enough to ship their wives across
the Atlantic to join them in homesteads scattered across the lonesome prairies.

The next immigrants were exiled Alsatian/Russian peasants
whose earlier kin had settled in North Dakota. They arrived by
way of Odessa and were escaping Stalin. But Stalin's influence
was not to be escaped. Near the end of the First World War,
Aberdeen became headquarters for the Red-leaning Industrial
Workers of the World (IWW), which was recruiting farmwork-
ers as well as miners and factory workers. By the 1920s, the town
was embroiled in a Populist agricultural reform movement that
ranged from the progressive Nonpartisan League in the Dakotas
to Soviet-led Marxist organizers in northeastern Montana, where
Plentywood's newspaper editor, sheriff, and legislative represen-
tative were Communists. But the revolution did not occur. Aberdeen's Home Guard vigilantes violently ousted the IWW, with
similar actions to follow in union towns such as Butte, Montana.

Aberdeen was also home to Hamlin Garland and Frank Baum,
plains writers whose work I've left behind in the crated memories
of childhood's library. I was never a fan of Hamlin Garland, but
Frank Baum's *Oz* books lined my bookshelf. Baum, I assumed,
was a Kansan like his heroine, Dorothy. Now I discover he was
his own model for the failed salesman who pretended to be a
wizard.

Baum arrived in Aberdeen in 1888 looking to start over after
failing as a theatrical producer and then as an oil salesman. He

bought a country store, which also failed, and the local newspaper, which he edited for a year. Baum witnessed the killer blizzard of '88 in South Dakota, and the drought that followed, and plenty of tempests. No wonder he dreamed of escape to an Emerald City. Some say he took a balloon ride at the Aberdeen state fair in 1890, which inspired him to imagine Dorothy and the Wizard's airborne return from Technicolor to black and white.

The fact that Kansas in the Oz books may actually be South Dakota sits in my stomach like undigested cholesterol. I tip the waitress, sure that Judy Garland's wide-eyed Dorothy never said, "Toto, we're not in *South Dakota* anymore!"

OUTBOUND
DAY THREE, MAY 13

Maps. Two-thirds of the way across the state, I still don't have a South Dakota road map. At a gas stop, I find a free one. To my eye, this map is a near mirror image of the ones for North Dakota, Nebraska, Iowa—even Kansas. The maps are similar because all this land was once a huge seabed carved by glaciers in repeated ice ages. When the glaciers retreated they dropped their sediments, blanketing the plains east of the 100th meridian in rich glacial soils called *loess*. That's the reason settlers were able to turn what once were tallgrass prairies into the "breadbasket" of the Midwest.

The prairie states' histories are not as interchangeable as their geographies. The politics of slavery divided them. Some were allied to the North during the Civil War. Others to the South. Such ties determined patterns of settlement and distributions of wealth and power. But in the long run, development on the Great Plains is ruled by prevailing winds, by rainfall, and by technologies that convert earth into energy.

The map's story is one of settlement. In the state's western quarter, a few highways divide blocks of white (grasslands and badlands) with secondary roads serving ranches and ranch towns. Broken-lined dirt tracks parallel blue veins of streams into the backcountry. Large green swatches denote national preserves and parks, including the Black Hills. Unroaded brown patches mark the state's seven Indian reservations. The Missouri River cuts through all of it like a fat blue worm. Eastward, the map's squares become smaller and crowded with grids—more towns, more roads—until words and lines jumble together along the Minnesota border.

Wonderful how history resides in our pathways and seems to slip away as we slip by, yet every mark we make is recorded on the map of our passing. Now I am passing from arid short-grass plains into the better-watered, red-brown soil of little bluestem country. More farmsteads appear. Wheat, barley, and oats replace hay and cattle. By afternoon Bruno and I will enter the Midwest's rich, moist agricultural heaven, where native species such as big bluestem have been displaced by a domesticated, mid-American grass called corn.

I turn south on I-29, my second interstate so far, which parallels Minnesota's western border. Bruno is crunched in the rear of the 4Runner below the open back window and between my duffel and his dog bag. "Hey, baby," I call to him. "How're you doing?" He ignores me. Drops his head on his paws. Sighs. My passenger is mad at me in the doleful, passive-aggressive way that is his trademark. There will be a rest stop past Waterton. "Soon, boy," I tell him. "Soon."

Lilacs. I pull in at the Waterton Auto Oasis. The air is humid and warm. Grass is lush green. A six-foot hedge of blooming purple lilacs separates the dog-run area from the cement-block lavatory and picnic grounds. Bruno zigzags along scent trails of pheasant or quail while I search for remains of the farmhouse that was here before the freeway. I find only lilacs. The original settler's wife must have planted these rows with their heart-shaped leaves—a woman in home-sewn gingham looking out at the prairie. Lonesome. Homesick. Longing for the perfume of an older world. I will plant a wall of lavender, she thinks, and it will keep me from blowing away.

Or perhaps the windbreak was a man's notion. A widower mourning his wife's death. He walks among the blossoms every May and remembers his love. Or maybe they were planted by a young man hoping to lure his beloved with a forest of flowers.

Deep purple French double lilacs were my flower of choice when I was in high school. My friends and I cruised alleys in Wilmette in my mother's red '53 Chevy convertible. We stole armloads of the fragrant fence-hugging branches to decorate our junior prom. Later, when I attended the University of Chicago, my soon-to-be husband, Dave Smith, and I used to kiss behind a tall lilac hedge behind the tennis court. Our passions were infused with the perfume of lilacs.

Speaking of passion, let me tell you more about the man who was my first and greatest love. But beware. Memory being the most self-serving of narrators, what follows may reveal more about me than about him. Nevertheless, anyone who knew Dave Smith would agree he was a charming, handsome, blue-eyed man of deep mood swings with a wicked sense of humor, a sharp mind, and an athlete's quickness and grace. He was an intellectual and a romantic whose quest for fulfillment led him from the practice of law to running the Washington State ACLU to becoming a PhD English professor, and finally, forsaking all the above, aspiring to be a filmmaker and a writer.

Although my complex and restless young husband had been filled with competing ambitions from his college days onward, he also harbored a simple desire for home and land. Montana was the spur. In the 1970s people like us could afford to buy some acres, own horses, and build a house by hand. So that's what we did. Despite failing health and a foreshortened future, Dave could be a rider of horses, a man on a tractor, a homesteader. Teenaged Eric, so closely tuned to his father he could tease him with impunity, reversed the usual father-to-son question: "What do you want to be when you grow up?" Dave answered with his ironic smile, "I want to be a cowboy!"

He wasn't the only one. I jumped at the chance to play woman homesteader—bandana instead of bonnet, worn Levi's, and muddy boots. I've written in previous books about how we bought the quarter-section of meadow and woods above Bear Creek. And how, when the original log house burned down before we could move into it, we crowded into a one-room bunkhouse and, with the help of friends, dismantled and rebuilt a two-story hewn-log house we'd found abandoned thirty miles up the Blackfoot. No need to repeat myself. What I want to stress here is Dave's vision and persistence. Sick as he was, he was the driving force. Eric and Steve, Dave's students and colleagues, my family, and our friends in Seattle put on overalls and joined in the work. Dave's homesteader dream swept all of us into a communal venture that changed our lives.

"Desire and pursuit of the whole," said Spinoza, "is called love." Dave was a lover in the Spinozan sense. He was a fine teacher, I've been told, but after years in the classroom, he wanted more. No one of his many accomplishments brought the satisfaction he craved. Dave Smith always wanted more.

We had been fans of the "new" cinema since the late fifties. Now Dave wanted to be a writer/director like Ingmar Bergman— an *auteur*. He taught Super 8 filmmaking through the English Department, organized a film series, and wrote script treatments. The black-and-white film we made in 1967 about Dick Hugo whetted his appetite, and by forty, although fatally ill, Dave was desperate to act out his fantasy. So once our house was chinked and the roof shingled, in the fall of 1973 he quit his tenured professorship. I urged him to just take a leave, but he was adamant. "I don't want no fuckin' bridges," said Dave (adapting our favorite line from *The Treasure of the Sierra Madre*). And like countless gold-seekers before, we set off that October for Los Angeles with no job and no insurance, chasing his Hollywood dream.

"You're crazy," said my mother on a long-distance call.

"I know," I replied, "but what the hell. What do we have to lose except time?"

We rented a shabby, one-bedroom furnished apartment in a transient's building a block behind Grauman's Chinese Theatre. The neighborhood was borderline slum and no longer exists, having been razed and replaced by an upscale shopping center. Our neighbors were mostly long-legged transvestites in hot pants and stacked heels, their false lashes thick with mascara. They moved out en masse one day and were replaced by black pimps schooling young blonde girls as eager as a bunch of cheerleaders.

In our tiny apartment with its red shag rug and fading brocaded wallpaper, Dave spent his mornings locked in the bedroom with his Olivetti on a makeshift desk. I see him there still, bundled in a blue terry-cloth bathrobe. His skin is sallow. Purple shadows circle his eyes. He is writing a sci-fi screenplay about the homeless street kids we see on our daily walks along Hollywood Boulevard. In his tale, they'll be shanghaied by a cult that preaches suicide as salvation and then uses the sacrificed kids as donors for black market organs. It was an idea whose time had not yet come, presaging Kazuo Ishiguro's novel *Never Let Me Go*—and the movie adapted from it.

After walking the twins to first grade in West Hollywood, I scoured ads in *Variety* and the *Hollywood Reporter* looking for jobs connected to what we called "the industry." Standing in line with drug dealers and whores at phone booths in the Hollywood Holiday Inn across the street (we couldn't afford a line of our own), I'd make futile calls to producers and studio execs. Then, in order not to disturb Dave, I hiked the Hollywood Hills. In my walkabout daydreams, Dave would sell his script, I would become a producer, the kids would go to private schools, and we'd live in a Spanish mansion draped in magenta bougainvillea with a tear-shaped pool in its courtyard, just like the ones I walked by every morning, occupied by mortals no prettier or smarter than me.

Our Hollywood pilgrimage ended as March ended, with a surge of homesickness and the urgent desire to witness spring in Montana. We packed our two suitcases of summer clothes, the twins' coloring books and toy soldiers, Steve's backpack and foam-rubber mattress, and Dave's Olivetti and scripts into our secondhand Ford, and headed for home. When we crossed Lookout Pass from Idaho into Montana, all of us were singing our favorite Woody Guthrie road song: *This land is your land / this land is my land / from California / to the New York island* . . . We were so happy to be coming home to our land.

Then, four days after his forty-first birthday, on May 8, 1974, Dave was irrigating our meadow—a thing he loved to do. It was a sunstruck afternoon, the meadow wet with runoff, brilliant with new grass, and popping with yellow buttercups and purple shooting stars. Happy in irrigating boots and mud-soaked jeans and making plans for a Memorial Day party, Dave came into our kitchen to wash hands before dinner. I see him there by the kitchen sink, turning to me with a surprised look. Always turning. Forever surprised. "Oh, dear," he said. Then he fell face-first to the maple floor, bloodying his nose. The six-year-old twins watched from the stairs while I tried to revive him with mouth-to-mouth resuscitation.

"You couldn't have done a thing," the doctor told me. "He was gone when he fell." Dave's heart just stopped. The cause was electrical failure—a condition called atrial fibrillation. He was only forty-one years old.

When it came time to bury him, two of my best friends and I decided to plant lilac bushes by Dave's grave. The grave had been dug in Missoula's old Catholic cemetery, a sloping hillside that falls below the freeway and looks over a working-class neigh-

borhood on the north side of the tracks. I chose to bury Dave
here, rather than in the newer cemetery, because this resting place
with mossy gravestones and mature, leafy trees has the air of permanence. And because across the street is a softball field where
some of our sporting writer friends and all of our sons played
city-league ball for a team called the Montana Review of Books.

Dave loved softball. We were sure he'd enjoy watching his sons
run the bases from a box seat in this haven where wide-branched
maples drop orange leaves in fall, where willows whisper in summer, and where in spring his personal lilac bushes would waft
their perfume over the earth where he lies.

"Dave would love to see us doing this," says Lucy, as we dig
through sod to plant the first young bush.

"Maybe he's watching us," I say to myself, wondering if his
newly freed spirit would be amused at our antics. Lucy and
Dave had bonded deeply in a mutual love of classical literature
during our rum-fueled, partying days of Seattle in the sixties.
Lucy is small and slender—athletic and quick—all that I am not.
She is Quaker, the mother of five, a grandmother to many, and
recently a great-grandmother. Now in her late eighties, she is still
a romantic in the classical mode, my hiking companion along
wilderness beaches, and a published poet at last. Lucy was the
first friend who caused me to be jealous. But I loved her when we
were young, and loved her that sad May in 1974 when Dave died,
and love her still.

"He loved all of us," says Anne, who has remained my best
friend for half a century. A tall, blonde, athletic woman with
ambitions to bring peace to the world, Anne was physically and
culturally more like Dave than I was, or Lucy, or Anne's geneticist
husband Dave, or Lucy's mountain-climbing husband Bill. Anne
was a leader of the peace movement in 1960s Seattle, when Dave
was running the Young Democrats and the Washington State
ACLU. Over the years she has become more deeply involved with

spiritual aspects of community healing than with conventional politics, but she was Dave's confidante. "He did it for you," she says, resting her hands on her shovel.

"What are you talking about?"

"The ranch. He wanted you to have something to hold onto after he was gone."

Anne is telling me that Dave wanted the log house we had built, and our quarter-section of meadow and forest, to be a sanctuary for me and the boys. He knew he would not live to see it finished and perfected. "Are you positive?" I say, my heart sinking. "I thought he built our place mostly to please himself."

Growing up poor in Depression-era Minnesota, an illegitimate child living with relatives, Dave had dreamed of owning land and horses—dreams I never had until I was in the midst of them. When we bought the ranch, I thought I was enabling him to live his fantasy, if only for a few years. But he recognized my attachment to that land and understood I would never leave it. He knew I would hold on to what I loved until I could grasp no longer. He knew me better than I know myself.

Anne and Lucy had come to Montana with their husbands a few days after Dave's funeral and burial. They wanted to help me in those eerie hours when death sinks in, and they wanted to hold their private ceremonies. They did not attend the funeral, but our four sons were there, and Pinky McNamara, from Minnesota, as well as Dave's half-brother, Johnny, his half-sister, Jenny, and his favorite aunt, Margaret. Dave's mother, Virtue, was too ill to come. Kathy had flown from New Jersey, and my parents from Chicago. Our Missoula writer friends had come in force—Dick and Ripley Hugo, Jim and Lois Welch, Jon Jackson, and many others. Carole, with her usual thoughtfulness, would visit a couple of weeks later. She knew that in my first days of shock and need I would be surrounded by loved ones, and then I would be alone.

In the frosty cemetery, Dick Hugo recited his eulogy over

Dave's grave. In part it reads: "David was happiest with the simple and immediate things others too often take for granted, his family, good friends, even grass, flowers, trees, animals. The part of him that suffered dissatisfaction was not as important as the part of him that lived as if just experiencing the world was enough. For him it often was."

Afterward, we did what Dave would have wanted us to do—drove back to the ranch, ate potluck food brought by neighbors and friends, played touch football with the big and little boys, drank wine and beer, and toasted Dave in the log house that many of those present had helped to build.

After all the guests but Kathy had gone home, the Seattle bunch arrived. We clustered in the open kitchen/dining area (there was no fireplace yet) and sang the folk songs we had sung on adventure-filled hikes along the Pacific Coast or around mountain campfires—guitars strumming as they had in days of youth and health: *When I'm on my journey, don't you weep after me* . . . and *Bring me a little water, Sylvie* . . . and *Goodnight, Irene* . . . The session ended with a circle dance—the Smith boys and Kathy, Anne and Dave, Lucy and Bill—holding hands, dancing, and singing along with the Nitty Gritty Dirt Band: *Will the circle be unbroken/ by and by . . . by and by.*

Over the next decade Dave would be joined in Missoula's Catholic cemetery by Dick Hugo, with a nook for Jim Welch and another for our house-building carpenter writer-partner Eric Johnson—all cut down in their prime. I like to imagine those aging boys emerging in moonlight among headstones of pioneers and nuns, war vets and babies dead from influenza. They are telling shaggy dog stories and raunchy jokes, laughing and drinking and playing ball. The party goes on without the rest of us. But some come to visit.

I arrive at the cemetery each May 8, with a bouquet of six red roses—one for each Smith—and a jar full of dogtooth violets and shooting stars picked from our meadow and woods. Eric and Becca usually drive down from Kalispell, combining commemoration and celebration, since Mother's Day comes right after Dave's birthday and death day. My birthday arrives on May 11, and Steve's is a week later, making May a month of weeping and laughter. Often Steve and Alex are there for the cemetery ritual, and these days Dave is visited by Andrew and his little girls, Tilly and Elodie. The girls race around gravestones or perch on Dave's black marble marker, sing songs, and pay scant attention as Andrew recites verses from Rilke.

It was lilac time in Missoula when Dave died, the city's bungalows and brick apartments framed with bushes taller than a footballer's head, its deserted lots lined with old plantings free for the taking. I have tried to grow lilacs by my house in the meadow, wanting flowering bushes like those in this lilac forest in Waterton Oasis, but I always fail. Once, I planted a lilac over the carcass of our German shepherd Sylvie. It withered and died. And I recently planted a shrub in a wet spot by our woodshed. It was nibbled to death by deer. Bill tells me my meadow is too cold for lilacs. But lilacs are the hardiest of species. Perhaps they are meant to exist on our Montana homestead only in my memory and imagination.

Now, at this rest stop near Minnesota's western border, the weight of moist air, the thick grass, and cloying fragrances tell me I have crossed from the prairies of adulthood into the heartland of my youth. I pick a handful of blossoms. No matter how these lilacs came to be, they move me to tears. Lilacs are for me a memorial to desire. I festoon the 4Runner's windshield with purple flowers. For a time briefer than first love, their sweetness will offset the pungent odor of western sage that droops from my rearview mirror.

Little House on the Prairie. Before departing, I study the tourist display by the parking lot. It describes the life and works of children's writer Laura Ingalls Wilder. The girl Laura, who was the main character in Wilder's books, was dear to me when I was little. She was not a dreamer or figment of fantasy like Dorothy in Oz, but a real girl with dirty feet, living gritty, and liking it. I knew Laura, but I did not know her maker. Now I learn that like her character, the author grew up poor and traveled the peripatetic road of a homesteader's daughter. Born in Wisconsin in 1867, she wandered with her Ma and Pa from Independence, Kansas, to Walnut Grove, Minnesota, to Burr Creek, Iowa, and finally to De Smet in South Dakota—the "little town on the prairie" some fifty miles west of where I stood. Laura lived there until she married a local farmer named Almanzo Wilder, and later moved with him to Mansfield, Missouri, in the Ozarks, where they ran their own family farm.

At age sixty-five in 1932, fighting grownup poverty and grieving after her parents' deaths, Laura turned to writing about her childhood. She remembered her nomadic years with no self-pity, calling them "wonderful" because they had given her experiences of frontier living that ranged from sod house to hotel, from farm to town. Wilder said she "wanted the children now to understand . . . what it is that made America as they know it." *Which children?* I wonder, thinking how childhood has changed. *And what America?*

The tough love of Wilder's prairie frontier; her heroine's affirmations of duty, hard work, and stoicism; and the rewards found in land, family, and community were values I absorbed from my immigrant parents and the culture at large in the 1940s. They would be useful years later to a young woman with a sick husband and four boys building her own homestead on a meadow in Montana. But what about my children? And the generations after them? They have grown up in an America more urban, comfortable, generous, greedy, populous, selfish, competitive, passive, homogeneous, diverse, and also more abstract. They and their children—even here in Montana—live in a post-nuclear age, in cyberspace and cars. Their world is thick with complexities of global proportions where Wilder's old-fashioned values are not necessarily useful. Laura's America is long gone, if it ever existed.

Even so, it is affirming for women past middle age to know it is possible to begin a new profession at sixty-five and reap success. When she began writing, Laura Wilder could not have guessed that her stories would hopscotch her to comfort and fame and give her a career that enabled her to work productively (with the writing help and marketing skills of her editor/daughter, Rose) through the next eleven years. Laura died when she was ninety, in 1957—well before her books became a television series that would make her heirs rich. But she never counted herself poor.

Leaving the rest area, I turn onto US 14, the Laura Ingalls Wilder Highway. This will be my yellow-brick road, passing me home to Chicago through the poppy fields of memory to 1943, when I was a pigtailed girl and seven years old. I had been quarantined that summer for six weeks after contracting polio on a Lake Michigan beach. This was at the height of a great epidemic, and I was sent to Michael Reese Children's Hospital in Chicago, which was overflowing with stricken children. Being bedded in a large crib was the first insult. "I'm a big girl," I complained to my parents. A big girl of seven should not be put in a bed with bars!

A few days later I would be forced to leave the beautiful contaminated toys my parents had brought—including a bride doll with a white dress and lace veil—leaving them for children not so lucky. The boy next to my crib was confined to an iron lung. He could not breathe without it, but he could talk to me.

"What's it like?" I asked.

"It doesn't hurt," he said.

On my other side was a girl with a paralyzed arm. I was humbled by the good cheer with which these children accepted their fates. It was my first lesson in the complexities of suffering. Had I stayed, I could have learned more, but since there was a dire short-age of beds and I was not paralyzed, the doctors sent me home.

I was bedridden most of that Indian summer, but on sunny afternoons I would be allowed to sit wrapped in my blanket in an overstuffed armchair on the glass-enclosed back porch of our third-floor apartment. Only my mother, pregnant with my youngest sister, Carole, was allowed to tend me. My sister Kathy had moved to another bedroom, my grandmother was ordered to keep her distance, and my father would poke his head into the door and talk to me each evening when he came home from work. But we could not roughhouse or play or touch one another.

I don't remember being unhappy, for even then I loved sol-itude. I amused myself with radio programs such as *The Lone Ranger* or *The Green Hornet*, which I was allowed to turn on for a few hours each day. I drew outside the lines in coloring books featuring Carmen Miranda and Roy Rogers and Trigger, and cut out paper dolls to enact dramas of romance and danger. But mostly I read books, including Laura Ingalls Wilder's prairie series. Sitting with one of those dove-covered illustrated volumes on my lap, I daydreamed about life on the prairie. There would be horses and dogs and deer, mountain lions, and wolves—animals I longed to have around me. The land would be open and as endless as Lake Michigan.

After I got well that fall, I pleaded with my parents to get a dog. No, they said. We cannot have a dog in the city. Our Chi-cago apartment house was guarded with stone lions. Kathy and I climbed them and rode them, the only pets we'd had except for an Easter rabbit named Pink Ears who escaped from our back-yard one spring day while we were taking him out for "exercise." I remember brick walls, a patch of weedy grass, a wishing well with no water, and the victory garden my father, Kathy, and I planted in a strip of shady, hard-packed dirt, four feet wide. Only radishes thrived in the dreary garden, and although we chased after Pink

Ears, we never saw him again. Kathy and I knew the world outside our garden wall was dangerous. This was 1943 and our country was at war. We knew the rabbit's escape meant being eaten by feral cats or loose dogs. We wept for Pink Ears, as little girls will.

Rats in the alley, trees in the park, squirrels, robins and pigeons, migrating geese, and gulls over Lake Michigan were as much of wild nature as I could find in Chicago outside of the Lincoln Park and Brookfield zoos, which by definition were not wild. It never occurred to me that life out west could be anything but fantasy. Or that one day I'd act out a version of Wilder's mama, raising four boys and a bunch of dogs and cats and horses in a log home on a Montana meadow where real wild animals—bear, coyote, elk, and deer—wandered free. Or that I would produce a movie about a Wyoming frontier woman named Elinore Stewart, whose high-plains story was harsher than the fictional Laura's.

The lesson of all this is be careful what you feed into a child's imagination. The nourishment they receive will influence their choices ever after.

Verdi. I have crossed into southwest Minnesota on the Laura Ingalls Wilder Highway 14 and feel the Midwest like rheumatism in my bones. The land changes from plains at Volga to rolling croplands pocked by lakes and ponds and patches of hardwood forests. I am charmed by tidy farms and leafy streets, the whitewashed towns, a yeoman's green kingdom. Whoa, I tell my sentimental self. You're a century too late. This sparsely populated farm country is all that remains of Jeffersonian paradise. Once it was the nation's heartland; now the young and restless have moved to cities or suburbs and paying jobs. The culture I would find here is closer to Garrison Keillor's Lake Wobegon or a senior citizen's Tea Party meeting or, more direly, Methland.

I'd like to detour to Verdi, a few miles off on a side road, a town even smaller than Volga. I assume it was named by an opera buff like my father, Steve Deutch. I try to imagine him striding across the plains as an immigrant settler but can't. Mom was the strider. My dad was a seer, a listener—a wiry, dark-haired, attentive fellow with a prominent nose, brooding brown eyes, and a sensuous mouth. He was likely to lurk in an alley with his camera, or position himself on a bench in the square where he could watch for the perfect lonely bench-sitter. More often than not, he'd make friends with his subjects: the turbaned holy man in India, or the old Greek woman leading her donkey, or the bleached blonde at the Beanie Weenie in Chicago.

Pista, as he was called (a nickname for Istvan, which translates to Stephen), was all his life a street kid: pugnacious, curious, hot-blooded. I knew his character, but not much of his personal history, because he told us very little about his childhood. Like many Jewish immigrants from central Europe, he wanted to be born again as an American—which meant leaving family stories of hard times and persecution back in the Old Country.

Having little factual history, I made up a story, imagining my father in a Hungarian version of Warsaw's ghetto, a crowded quarter of pogroms and segregation like those I'd seen in Holocaust movies. When he read my interpretation of his early life in one of my first published essays, my father laughed. Pest, he said, had a Jewish neighborhood but did not have a ghetto. (Except the ghetto set up by German occupying troops near the end of World War II when my father was long gone.)

"You've got it wrong. All wrong. I grew up in the heart of the city. On the main street. It was like living on the Champs Élysées . . . or Michigan Avenue."

Michigan Avenue? I could hardly believe that story. But I found it was true when I traveled to Budapest after my father died. The apartment building on Andrássy Avenue where he had grown up in a crowded janitor's apartment with his father, mother, and two older brothers was located in the swinging center of Hungarian culture at its *fin de siècle* apex. The State Opera House was a block away, and the theater district two blocks up the avenue. Also the State Dance Academy, Liszt's piano studio, and fashionable restaurants and cafés. The Jewish quarter's narrow streets ran helter-skelter on one side of the avenue, merging at the ornate Dohány Synagogue. The other side led to the city's mammoth Catholic basilica. And chugging under the middle of the extra-wide avenue was the world's first subway.

I imagine my father and his brothers roaming the neighborhoods from Heroes Square to Museum Street and the old university quarter by the Danube. They loiter outside cafés where intellectuals congregate, swipe oranges from outdoor markets, play pickup soccer, and gape at the theater crowds. In an era when street life was a main source of communication, these three sons of a Jewish janitor picked up ideas and fashions and visions of the arts that would incite each to become an artist.

Pista, my mother tells me in one of her favorite stories, loved to stand outside the Opera catching drifts of melody that wafted through open side doors on warm evenings. "Once, your daddy threw out his shoulder, he was conducting so hard." She laughs.

Mom's stories are tinged with her sense of the ridiculous, the comic, the frivolous. Dad was more serious. Even his jokes had an edge of bitterness or irony. Snapshots in our family album show him as a skinny kid with shaved head and protruding ears. His posture is rebellious. A spark of mischief gleams in his eyes. I imagine that child standing alongside the Opera House. He has escaped his father's strict eye, his mother's chores, and the odious duty of going to synagogue. He is enraptured by the singing, the spectacle. People stare at the odd kid who is humming and waving his arms. Pista doesn't notice. He is a conductor. This is Verdi!

My father never grew out of his conductor phase. I see him in our living room in Chicago, and later in our house in Wilmette, at ease on Sunday mornings. The stereo is turned up loud to a Beethoven symphony or a Mozart concerto or a Bach string quartet. Pista is wearing a worn, checkered flannel shirt. He has not shaved. His eyes are closed. He is humming or whistling or singing bits of melody. His arms move vigorously to the music.

When I was eleven, my father took me and Kathy to see *Aida* at the Chicago Lyric Opera. I cannot remember what impressed me more, the live camels or the heroine's Egyptian headdresses. Certainly not Verdi. My parents made me take piano lessons. Their good friend Margit Varro had been a star pupil of Bartók's in Hungary, but even she could not turn my awkward hands and tin ear toward musical accomplishment. Although I loved Bach and Mozart and Irving Berlin and Fats Waller, I would never master the piano. My father was equally inept. He began to take lessons from Madame Varro in his forties, determined to realize his dream of making music with his own hands. I remember him practicing on our upright Steinway every evening when he came home from his photographic studio. But his fingers were stiff and clumsy, coarsened by the chemicals he used to develop negatives and prints in his darkroom, and he gave up in frustration.

As I drive between Volga and Balaton, I flip through my CDs and find Verdi's *Requiem*, composed to honor Italy's poet Alessandro Manzoni and Verdi's mentor Rossini. The music begins. The requiem soars. My father's face appears in my mind. His eyes are shut tight, and there are no lines of age or experience to mar the white mask of his visage—a vision of deathlike rapture that duplicates exactly the plaster mask he made of himself as a young sculptor in Paris.

Song fills the Toyota. I roll down the window to let some of the sound out. I turn the volume up. Here comes the *Dies Irae:* "The day of wrath, that day shall / Dissolve the world in ash." I push the repeat button. "*Lacrimosa dies illa:* That day is one of weeping on which shall rise again from the ashes the guilty man, to be judged."

Lacrimosa. Tears. My father's face dissolves in tears. He was a man not ashamed to weep. Music could move him to tears at home, but also in a crowded concert hall. I would sit next to him in Orchestra Hall at a piano recital or string quartet and observe the tears coursing down his cheeks. Self-conscious and inhibited by social norms, I cringed at his display of pure emotion, wondering why I was not moved to such extremes. *Pista.* Stripped naked before me and the entire world.

I can think of no syllables more suitable as tribute and lament for my father than Verdi's *Requiem*: "Spare then this one, O God." But his longtime friend and leftie fellow traveler, Studs Terkel, offered a different kind of tribute. Studs spoke at my father's memorial service in 1997 in the chapel at the University of Chicago where I had married Dave Smith in 1955. Master of the bon mot, fluent, and needing no notes, he characterized my father precisely.

> Well, this is Steve Deutch. It's no accident he was a close and dear friend of Nelson Algren, because both of them were pursuing that world *beyond* the billboards, that lone person on that park bench, the anonymous out there. . . . There was Budapest, there was Paris, but Chicago . . . I quote Nelson [Algren], Steve's closest friend: "[Being part of] Chicago is like being married to a woman with a broken nose. There may be lovelier lovelies. But never a lovely so real." And that's Steve's gift, catching the realness, the truth, no matter what.

Balaton. When I see Balaton on the main route's signpost I know I must stop there instead of sidetracking to Verdi. The original Balaton is a fifty-mile-long lake in Hungary so large it is called the Hungarian Sea. This is as near as Hungary gets to sea, for the land of my ancestors is a landlocked plain with mountains at its borders and the blue Danube running through it.

Hungarians visit Balaton's resorts to enjoy the fairy-tale countryside, see villages where ruins of fortresses date back to the
thirteenth century, and inspect the crypt of King András I, which
was built in 1055. My forbears on my father's side—the Deutschs
and Brauns—were Jewish cobblers and working folk from small
towns who landed in Budapest, too poor and oppressed or too
class bound and religion bound to have ventured as tourists into
the gentile hinterlands. And although my mother's father was an
insurance executive in Transylvania who could afford to travel,
he did not take his family to visit vineyards along the lake or sun
themselves in a cove along miles of sandy beaches. They could
have climbed volcanic cliffs of black basalt, seen yacht clubs
where sailboats raced, or boarded a steamboat ferry from port
to port. But according to my mother, they did not vacation in
Balaton.

Artists and poets lived along Balaton's shores. And composers,
rich people, and peasants tied to the land. If Jews were allowed
into Lake Balaton's fancy spas (I suspect they were not), my
grandparents might have taken their aged mothers and fathers
to soak their aches away and drink curing waters in the mineral
hot springs, as they did in the city. Hot springs and spas found
all along the Danube's Hungarian shores have been a source of
recreation and healing from prehistory to Roman times, from
the Ottomans to the Hapsburgs, and through the Stalin era until
now, but following the "Jewish laws" of 1920 until after World
War II, Jews were allowed to bathe only in special "Jewish" pools.

In the United States there were no such restrictions. The first
spa I ever stepped into was in St. Joseph, Michigan, about twenty
miles north up the lake from our summerhouse in Sawyer. My
parents would take my grandmothers there "to take the waters"
when they were sore of bone and in need of refreshment. I remember a Victorian lobby with ferns and Oriental rugs and the first
parrot I could get close to. I would hold out a piece of bread, and

the big green bird on his perch would cock his moth-eaten head, look at me with a sardonic eye, and say "Polly wants a cracker."

The Balaton I find now along a small lake in western Minnesota does not evoke its namesake. The town fathers who named it might have been joking. Or perhaps they were so homesick they gave the same name to dissimilar places. I assume the namers were Hungarian, but discover that most of the immigrants in this region were German, with Norwegians following close behind. Who knows why they named their town after a huge lake in Hungary.

One thing I do know is if some of those settlers were Hungarian, farming was deep in their culture. I had not realized how deep until I read in Richard Manning's book, *Against the Grain: How Agriculture Has Hijacked Civilization,* that the Hungarian plain—a land of rich loess soils like those of the Midwest—is one of the oldest agricultural settlements in Europe. Pottery shards and artifacts of farming dug up there by archaeologists date back six thousand years. Scientists surmise that these technologies were carried from the Tigris and Euphrates valleys to the Caucasus and then west through Eurasian grasslands by fierce tribes who drove indigenous hunters and gatherers to the edges of extinction.

I try to imagine an elderly Hungarian woman in western Minnesota at the end of the nineteenth century. What would she do without smoked salamis hanging from beams? Or bright bunches of red peppers to be ground into paprika? There would be no golden Tokaj wine in the cellar, or the many-layered, chocolate cream-filled *Dobos torte* my grandmother Beck made on special occasions, complete with a glassy, brown, burnt-sugar icing. If the immigrant had come from a large town on the plains like the ones my grandmother Beck inhabited, she would find no Gothic cathedrals on this prairie, no concert hall where she might hear Liszt or Verdi on a Saturday night, no domed synagogues. I doubt that these green pastures, this pond-sized lake, the few fellow immigrants who could understand her language would be sufficient company. She would have felt displaced, as my mother's mother must have felt when she came to Chicago in 1938—a gracious woman, sad at heart, living through her children and grandchildren and, unlike her ambitious daughter and son-in-law, homesick.

Deciding to forego the broasted chicken special at the roadside café, I let Bruno out for a run in the lakeside park with its Victorian cupola. While he takes a blissful dip, I sit on a bench and call my mother on the cell phone.

"I'm in Balaton," I say. The connection crackles. I can almost see my mother roused from her nap on the couch, blinking her eyes and adjusting her hearing aids.

"Where?"

"Balaton, like in Hungary. I thought it'd be fun to call you from Balaton."

"Where are you? My hearing aid is bad. Wait. I'll try to change it."

"I'm in Minnesota." I shout. My elaborate plan to speak to her of Balaton goes down the toilet.

"Oh, good. When will you get here?"

"Not till tonight. I've got a long way to go. I'll call you after dinner, when I know better."

"All right, darling." Mom is wide-awake now and into her fussing mode. "Aren't you tired? I'm worried about you . . . so much driving."

"I'm fine." It's time to stop this too familiar conversation. "See you soon."

I must be smiling to myself, for an elderly gentleman passing by smiles in return. I am smiling because there is something comic about a daughter nearing seventy reassuring her almost hundred-year-old mother that she is all right. What I don't realize is that

I have filled my mother with false hope. *Soon* is a relative word. I may have arrived in the Midwest, but I'm far away from Chicago.

A River to Cross. I stop for gas on the Minnesota side of the Mississippi. Looking across the bridge that will carry me over the river to La Crosse in Wisconsin, I recognize my country of young love. Here is a shoreline of brush and trees so dense it seems a solid thing. There are greens in twelve variations. Splatters of mauve. Surprising purples. Just a few miles upstream there once was a shabby crossroads motel—a sacred funny place, likely long gone—where I spent my first night on the road with a lover.

It is June 1954. School is over and summer has begun. Dave Smith and I are driving to Minnesota in my mother's new yellow Chevy convertible. The top is down. My cropped hair, black and curly, does not blow in the wind. His brush cut shines blond in the sun. Dave is taking me to meet his aunts, uncles, and cousins in Hastings, Minnesota, where he had grown up under their care.

"We'll be staying with Aunt Marg," we told my parents— Marg, the youngest and worldliest of the seven Smith sisters and the closest to Dave. But we did not tell them we planned to arrive at Marg's the next day.

"Let's get a ring," I say. At eighteen I am nervous about checking into a motel with a man. We stop at a Woolworth's. The fake jewels are crude and obvious so we settle on a packet of rings made for hanging lace curtains. I slip one on my ring finger. It's too big, but plain and gold colored.

The pimply-faced desk clerk barely glances at me, much less my left hand. "A room for my wife and me," says Dave.

"Facing the river, if it's not too expensive," I pipe in, mimicking my mother, who always bargained for something better.

In our small, cheap waterfront room, mosquitoes and june bugs batter the screened windows. The Mississippi, running high in spring flood, envelops us in a constant thrum. Being alone in our own private place is new and exciting—much better than the backseat of my mother's car or rolling on a dark beach in Sawyer, where my sisters or parents might stumble over us. Dave and I are covered with road dust and sweaty, so we dump our clothes and make slippery, dripping, laughing love in the shower. That night we snuggle close, and I fall into sleep with Dave's arm around me, his scent on the pillow. We wake before dawn, groping for each other in morning lust. Our mating is slow and sinuous, and we fall back to sleep serenaded by calls of awakening birds and the never-ending rush of the great river.

As we drive toward Hastings I am anxious. What will Dave's Baptist, all-American, rural relatives think of me, an immigrant Jewish girl from the city? What can I say to them, with no common interests except David? Some of his aunts and uncles have traveled to Hastings from southern Illinois and Wisconsin to meet Dave's girl—it's a serious occasion. I've got to put on my best face. But no—as if to fulfill my negative expectations—that evening at his aunt Grace's house, the first thing I do is break the rules.

Following the custom of the country, Dave's aunts and his cousin Cora have crowded into the ample kitchen of Grace's two-story white frame house. The men are in the living room, sitting in armchairs and sipping iced teas, while grandkids and cousins romp with a dog in the large fenced yard. The women are peeling potatoes and cleaning chickens, preparing green beans from the garden for the evening meal. A couple of fragrant apple pies cool on a windowsill.

"What can I do to help?" I ask.

"Not a thing, dear. Just make yourself to home."

I lean against a wall wearing the fashionable madras plaid Bermuda shorts my mother has bought me to take to college. No one else is wearing shorts. Or madras. The older ladies wear dresses and aprons; the younger ones wear pressed cotton slacks. I listen to gossip about folks I don't know and children I care nothing about. Awkward and out of place, I wander into the living room where men are talking politics and sports—subjects that actually interest me. I sit on the floor by Dave's chair. The uncles look at me and then away from me. All talk stops. Dave makes some kind of crack that causes them to laugh. I wish I could remember what he said, but I was too embarrassed to remember anything but my embarrassment. He puts his arm around my shoulder. Talk resumes.

A few years after Dave's death, his mother, Virtue, the black sheep and outcast of her family, was committed to a state insane asylum in that same town. Diagnosed with schizophrenia, violent and catatonic, she died under suspicious circumstances while being operated on for a broken arm. Since then we've kept in touch with Dave's half-sister Jenny, who took care of her mother until it was no longer possible, and his half-brothers Johnny and Lester (all born of different fathers), but have lost contact with the rest of the Smith clan. Only Aunt Marg and Dave's favorite cousin, Howie, would write or visit us; and when Marg passed away in old age, communications almost stopped.

Although Dave and I took the boys to see Aunt Marg and her family at their pony farm outside Hastings and occasionally visited his older aunts in small towns in Michigan, Wisconsin, and Minnesota, I felt like a stranger to Grace and Beulah and Flossie and Mary and Maebelle—separated by distance and culture, religion and politics, and just plain indifference. It may be my fault that the blood link was severed after Dave died, but he is also to blame, for Dave divorced himself from most of his aunts and his uncle when they rejected his mother—even though he, too, could not live with her craziness. The distance began much earlier, when he went to the University of Chicago to become a lawyer; it grew when he went to Seattle to practice law and then to get a PhD; and the last tenuous bonds were broken in Missoula, where Dave was a professor and an intellectual and sixties rebel with no ties to the conservative and religious cultures of his Midwestern relatives. I'm sure his children must have sensed his feelings, but it's equally likely our sons have neglected contact with many relatives on their Smith side because of entropy. The simplest answer is that my family, the tightly bound artistic and urban Deutch family, has nurtured a circle so compelling that it devours all energies available for clandom.

All that remains of my first contact with Dave's homeland are memories and a keepsake. There is a green leather jewelry box crammed into an oak cabinet next to my bed. It dates back to my high school years and contains a bunch of sentimental junk, including the false wedding ring that Dave and I fooled no one with when I was eighteen. It also harbors the gold wedding band I wore during our nineteen-year marriage. The false ring and the real ring rest side by side in a velvet-lined compartment along with Dave's Psi U fraternity pin and my uncle Paul Deutch's Purple Heart.

Nighttime Freeways. There is no need to describe the fast-as-I-can-go sunset drive on I-90 through Madison, Wisconsin, where my youngest sister, Carole, went to college and where I can find no place to eat near the freeway. Or my disappointment in seeing the souvenir arcades with life-sized wooden Indians, or garish dinosaur parks, or faux Gothic castles where tourists play miniature golf in Wisconsin Dells.

My single memory of the Dells takes place in an oversize canoe. I am four or five years old. We ride the river between stone cliffs. There is a waterfall. A real Indian in a feathered headdress pilots the boat. In the story I have made from that image, Mother worries I might tumble overboard. Father points his Rolleiflex at the sights. Uncle Gene rides with us. I'm not sure if he was actually there or if I added him to this memory because I adored him, dark-eyed and teasing, tossing me into the air, *hoop-la.*

Another flash of Wisconsin. One of my earliest memories. I

am with my mother and father, my baby sister, Kathy, and my grandparents Deutch. We are staying at a guest-farm. The barnyard chickens smell nasty. They scratch in the dirt with horny feet. I am afraid of their wings. There is a spotted milk cow, black and white, with a gigantic swinging udder. I pet the baby lambs, wondrous to a three-year-old who lives in an apartment on Chicago's North Side. The air is hot and muggy. Wet grass is squiggly between bare toes. I hold tight to my grandmother's hand. It is plump and comforting like her soft lap, the sweet/sour smell of her.

This evening as I drive the Wisconsin freeway, Grandma Deutch's scent seems to hover above my left shoulder. Violets and sweat meld with talcum powder. Her perfume is as tangible as the dust drifting into my car's window. I regret that I didn't know her more intimately. That I didn't quiz her about her childhood and ancestors in what is now the Czech Republic. Or her unhappy marriage to my grandfather, Julius. I should have begged her to tell stories about my father and his brothers in Budapest. Should have prodded her to talk about emigrating to Chicago. Even daring to ask what drove her to settle in the city where her eldest son had died. But I didn't.

Honi-nani, as she was called (a nickname for Aunt Johanna that I interpreted as Aunt Honey), was a sharp-tongued, ironic, round little woman with no discernible neck, whose humor delighted me as much as her matzo-ball soup and Hungarian cookies. Her round brown eyes, magnified through heavy lenses, made her look owlish but sparkled with intelligence. I felt more kinship to her than to my soft-hearted, genteel, sad, and nagging live-in Grandma Beck. And I still do.

Day darkens. I put the last chapters of *The Life of Pi* on the tape deck. The story of a boy and tiger bound together in a lifeboat and drifting aimlessly across the Pacific is a story I connect to. I, too, am drifting. My sea is the industrial wastelands surrounding the freeway. And there is a furry beast in my vessel. He snores gently behind the driver's seat. We are floating at seventy-five miles per hour.

Mom calls on my cell phone, worried, and I tell her I'll be there around ten o'clock. She sighs. It is getting past her bedtime, but I'm going as fast as I can. I am nearly out of gas and hungry, so I pull off at a brightly lit freeway island, gas up, buy a stale chocolate doughnut and black, bitter coffee, and return to Pi's multiple ending. When we reach the exit to O'Hare Airport, his story is over and I am beginning a new chapter in mine. It will be thirty minutes to touchdown.

I turn east off I-90 at the Lawrence Street exit. Bruno raises his head when we come to stoplights as if to ask, childlike, *Are we there yet?* or *I have to go to the bathroom.* We drive east toward Lake Michigan, passing Polish and Slavic neighborhoods near the freeway. Further along we enter more recent émigré regions marked with signs in Arabic, Korean, Chinese, and Vietnamese. The grimy buildings are two or three stories, some with bay windows, some with front stoops, and most are made of red or yellow brick—the building blocks of choice when the charred wooden city was rebuilt after the 1871 Chicago fire.

We approach Clark Street and come to the cemetery in which the ashes of my grandparents Deutch and grandmother Beck, and perhaps my uncle Alfred, are stored in forgotten vaults. I will have to ask my mother where I could find them if I came looking. Unless we sisters keep track, after Mom is gone, no one will remember to honor these blood migrants who rest far from the lands where their ancestors are buried. Sometimes I doubt if it matters where anyone is buried. Dust to dust and all that. And sometimes I believe that it does. Burial grounds are storehouses for memory. And memory matters, no matter how skewed.

We enter the neighborhood I grew up in, and the familiar dimly lit streets seem haunted, shabby, and diminished—a different neighborhood than the one I recall. I wonder if the Granada Cinema on Clark Street—where Grandma Deutch took Kathy and me to see Marx Brothers comedies, Tyrone Power costume dramas, Zachary Scott westerns, and sweetie-pie Shirley Temple movies—is still open. I know the fishmonger's store where she bought smoked Lake Superior whitefish no longer exists. And the butcher shop where Grandma Beck chose chickens to be killed on the spot is also gone. The caged white leghorns stank of excrement and fear. They disgusted me in childhood and again when we tried to raise them on our Montana homestead, but even in the heart of this city that spawned me I learned early that killing animals for meat is what people like us must do if we wanted to enjoy chicken paprika, or liver pâté, or barbecued rib eyes, or smoked whitefish on rye bread with cream cheese or sour cream.

Becoming vegetarian was not a possible choice. We were Hungarian Jews of common stock and thought vegetarians were abnormal. Like the Vietnamese whose restaurants line my path to Sheridan Road, my family devoured every part of our prey. Even the scaly chicken feet. I see them floating yellow with long nails in the fatty broth of Grandma Deutch's chicken and dumpling soup. Feet so ugly. Vivid and necessary.

THE BREAKERS

NIGHT THREE / MORNING FOUR, MAY 13–14

The Breakers. I turn into the circular driveway of the Breakers, a glass-walled skyscraper thirty-four floors high on the lake side of Sheridan Road, just north of Foster. This is an apartment residence for old people who are able to care for themselves or hire their own help. And this is where my mother has lived since my father died in 1997. Her neighbors are mostly Jewish widows or Irish Catholic widows and, like her, well enough off to end their days in comparative luxury. Mom's one-bedroom flat is on the thirty-second floor, with views over Lake Michigan and south to the Loop's skyscrapers. I bet she is standing near her bay windows looking out at the revolving lights on the Ferris wheel at the tip of Navy Pier. The television is on, but she pays it no heed.

I pull into the building's underground garage. Bruno peers warily from the tailgate. I have to yank him by the collar to get him down. He hates being underground. He will not drink when I pour my last half-bottle of water into his dish. He gives me a baleful look, as if to say, "What the hell have you gotten me into this time?"

I put his choke chain around his neck and he lets me lead him toward the elevator that will take us to street level. But when the steel door to the creaky coffin-like box clanks open, he plants his feet, lowers his head, and will not move. I can't budge him or bribe him. Leaden with resistance, his ninety-four pounds seem like two hundred. The hairs on his back rise, ready for attack. What can I do? Bruno needs to relieve himself before I lock him into the car for the night. I spot a man heading toward the red EXIT light in a far corner of the garage. We follow him. A heavy metal door opens into fresh air. Bruno yanks me up the stairway toward the street. I lean back, reining him in like a horse. I hear the deadbolt click shut behind us. Damn it to hell. We are locked out.

Bruno tugs at his leash and I can't hold him any longer. We dash toward the park that adjoins the Breakers. At night the place is nearly deserted and possibly dangerous, but there is a police person in a patrol car near its entrance and a few other dog people are doing what I'm doing. When the other dogs are gone, I release Bruno. He runs round and round on the mown grass, sniffs and marks territory by a flowering crabapple. After ten minutes of freedom, I drag him toward the circular drive at the main entrance to the Breakers.

Jerome, the tall, graying, mustachioed doorman from Aruba knows me from previous visits, but steps back at the sight of my big brown dog. Bruno jumps up at him, wags his tail. "Down, boy," I grab his collar. "Down!"

The doorman pats Bruno on the head. I ask if I can take Bruno up to my mother's apartment. I know Jerome is solicitous toward her, and she is fond of him. "She's expecting us. She loves this dog." He raises his eyebrows. "Call her yourself, you'll see." Jerome is hesitant, so I fall into begging mode. I'm sure I look pitiful—a woman well past middle age in worn jeans and dirty T-shirt with white shaggy hair and baggy, bleary eyes. I clasp my hands in a praying position. "He won't go back down in that garage. It scares him to death."

The doorman relents. We enter the revolving door into the exterior lobby. It has marble floors, upholstered chairs, and couches where residents wait for visitors or watch the comings and goings of cars and taxis in the mobile world. A security guard stands behind the entrance window. He wears a uniform complete with holster and gun, and his light brown face is sprinkled with dark freckles. When I remind him that I am Mrs. Deutch's eldest daughter—the one from Montana—who has driven across the plains to Chicago and is pure exhausted, he unlocks the glass door to the interior lobby and comes out of his cubbyhole to look us over. Now Bruno wants to jump up on the security guard's chest.

"Is he vicious?"

"Does he look vicious to you?"

Bruno smiles his dog smile. He is wagging all over, a "Coco puff," as my dog-sitter, Buzzy, calls him. The two men grin at me and my brown dog. They take turns petting him. The lobby is deserted. We are a diversion from the tedium of night watch or the sadness of an ambulance arriving at 3 a.m. to pick up an oldster with a heart attack or, worse still, the exit of a warm corpse.

"Just be sure to get him out of here early, before the old peoples sees him and gets scared," says the security guard.

"You bet." I head for the elevators. "Thank you so much."

One elevator stands open. It is ample and carpeted. A prod in the butt gets Bruno inside. He looks at me with a quizzical expression while we are whisked to the thirty-second floor, and then he walks out as if he rides elevators every day.

Apartments. I knock on the door to 32L. As soon as Mom opens it a crack, Bruno jumps up to greet her. I have to pull him back hard to keep him from knocking her down. Bruno on two feet is nearly as tall as my mother. I lean down to receive her kiss. She is soft-skinned, fragrant with Miss Dior cologne, dressed in off-white slacks and a blue blouse, and her cheeks are pink with rouge. Mother has shrunk from her mature height of a little over five feet to about four feet, ten inches, and has a mildly humped back. Her cropped hair is white and carefully waved. Although she bemoans her wrinkles, she looks much younger than ninety-seven.

Bruno won't be satisfied until he gives Mom a kiss. She has known him since he was a four-month-old fur ball in Montana. "I love that dog," she says, patting his head. He rolls over on his back, legs in the air. She rubs his tummy. It causes him to wiggle his back leg uncontrollably.

Entering the hallway, I rest my hand on the bird's-eye maple cabinet I have known all my life and feel immediately at home. This one-bedroom flat with creamy walls and carpets is a distilled version of apartments my parents had occupied for half a century or more. Only once did they desert the city to buy a white stucco house in Wilmette, and although their suburban idyll lasted ten years, it ended in divorce and eventual remarriage—a story I will not digress to tell now. Then, for the next thirty years, until my father died at eighty-nine, my parents returned to the urban apartment life.

From the Montparnasse apartment/studio where I was born to this high-rise old-folks' retreat, all the apartments my parents inhabited have had the same ambience: large windows look down to a park or lake or cityscape; the desks and cabinets are modern style from the thirties, forties, and fifties, designed by my father or Herman Miller; chairs are Eames; sofas, Danish Modern, upholstered (often by my mother) in fabrics designed by Frank Lloyd Wright and his ilk. White walls are hung with my father's framed black-and-white photographs of nudes and his color prints from travels abroad: there is a holy man in Delhi; Malian dancers; a bench-sitter in Paris. His wooden sculptures in curvy Henry Moore shapes rest on end tables and pedestals. My uncle Gene's ceramic lamps and swan-shaped bowls sit on every surface and drip with glazes in colors of earth and sky. There are paintings by friends such as Aaron Bohrad and shelves stacked with art books; a stereo and a fine collection of classical music; and artifacts from trips around the world—Turkish rugs, Japanese figurines, flowered Mexican vases, and a primitive-style painting of Polish peasant sisters.

We enter the living room with its rose-colored couch and sit by the glass-topped coffee table whose wooden base was carved by my father. Mother asks if I am hungry. I nod, but before I take a bite I pour myself a double shot of the Jack Daniel's my sister Kat has stashed in a kitchen cupboard. Then I smear a glob of *kurozott* on a cracker. This is a Hungarian cheese spread that is Mother's ritual homecoming dish. Made of cream cheese and butter, it is salmon pink from spoonfuls of paprika, dotted with rounds of green onion, and speckled with caraway seeds.

She holds one out to Bruno. He snaps it into his pink-lipped mouth. "No more cheese," I say. He looks at her, not me. She gives him another cracker, then a third. Bruno regards Mom with adoring yellow eyes, waiting for the fourth.

"Stop begging," I tell him. He puts his head down on his paws.

My mother lives for her children, grandchildren, and great-grandchildren, and family is what we talk about until past midnight. Her coffee table, end tables, and bureaus are busy with framed photographs and albums. Mom's hearing is almost gone, and though her eyes still work pretty well, she can't focus her mind on reading books. But she loves to look at the photos we send her and entertains herself by making up conversations among great-grandbabies she barely knows. Although most are too young to speak, they speak to her. She records their imagined words on Post-it notes colored lime green and fuchsia. I find a few stuck to the coffee table next to framed pictures of baby Joaquin in San Francisco and baby Tilly in Montana and toddler Iris in Los Angeles: *Hi Joaquin. Want to kiss me?* And *Tilly, Tilly, your name is silly!* And *Iris loves her kitty. Do you love your Mommy?*

As the clock moves toward midnight, we chat about who is

working and who is not—a necessary question when several of Mom's daughters and grandchildren have been on unemployment or are freelance writers or filmmakers living on the edges of poverty. Eric, my eldest son, is the exception. Until the housing bubble exploded in 2008 (several years after this visit), Eric made a good living selling houses and land in Montana's Flathead Valley. "The only person in this family," he crowed at my father's memorial service, "who pays *into* Social Security!"

Finally, it is time for Mom to do her ablutions, a routine that will take about an hour. She is obsessive about scrubbing her false teeth. Obsessive about splashing cold water onto her cheeks over and over again because she read in a beauty magazine that repeated watering would free her face from wrinkles. She combs her white hair for about ten minutes, until it lies in waves just the way she wants it. While she performs her bathroom rituals, I return to the garage, grab my backpack, Bruno's dog dish and food, and his rug from the back of the SUV. By the time he is settled below the open living room window, it is my turn to use the facilities.

Tonight I sleep in the twin bed by the walk-in closet in Mom's bedroom, about three feet from her matching bed, too close for comfort. I hear her labored breathing, a gurgle coming up in her throat that would alarm me on nights when I am not so exhausted. But this night my head settles on the hypoallergenic too-hard pillow. I fall into heavy sleep, not waking until a wet nose brushes my hand. Bruno is telling me the sun has risen. Sure enough, stripes of yellow light flare through the venetian blinds. I hear the roar of morning rush-hour traffic on the Outer Drive.

Safe Harbor. Bruno handles himself with aplomb this morning, walking into the empty elevator with no resistance. But it is later than I had planned, and the breakfast crowd is at its peak. On our way down, the elevator stops a dozen times for elders going to breakfast or heading to exercise classes. Most of the residents wear blazers or patterned sweaters, and there's lots of gold jewelry. Ladies are heavily made up and sport the beauty-shop look de rigueur for seniors: white hair cropped short and curled; or hennaed waves ranging from flaxen to copper. A few (cancer victims or not) are topped with glossy wigs. Many smile. The hopeless stare blank-faced at the elevator door. But even they are surprised to see a huge male dog with yellow eyes sitting alertly in the rear corner.

"Nice doggie," says a skeletally thin woman. She grabs her walker with one hand and strokes Bruno's head with the other.

"Is he friendly?" asks a bent, bald man holding out trembling fingers.

A pretty African American nurse's aide steps into the elevator, spots Bruno, utters a cry, almost drops her tray, and jerks back as if burned. We thread through the lobby and reach the revolving exit door without barks, growls, or knocking down old folks.

The wind off Lake Michigan is a Windy City slap in the face. It whips around the semicircular entrance to the Breakers and wakes me out of the funk this warehouse for the elderly brings on. I realize I've been holding my breath. Why does this posh high-rise infect me with stress and fear? It haunts me in deeper ways than intensive care units or nursing homes where dying is imminent and visible.

Bruno pulls me through the tunnel under the Outer Drive that links the Breakers' park to the lakeshore. It's all been thought out. Flowering trees, green spaces, the ever-changing lake she loves are as easy for my mother to access as the dining room where she eats breakfast and dinner. Tomorrow she will take me by the hand and lead me to her favorite bench by a crabapple tree. The tree is full of birds. I'm not an expert and it's too dark to tell what they are. Perhaps nutcrackers or blackbirds, an occasional crow. When the sky turns purple, the birds will rise noisily from their branches and fly upward in a V-shaped formation. That's when the jets come screaming overhead, contrails marking a sky path over the lake.

"See," says Mom, "the birds are showing the way. They are telling the airplanes where to go." She studies the air and nods her head. "It's my secret," she whispers. "I watch the birds every evening, and every evening they are here. And when they have done their job with the airplanes, then they fly away."

I wonder if my mother is losing her mind. Or if she is simply escaping into a personal mysticism rooted in the natural world. Here is her bench for meditation, a patch of grass, some flowers, and a tree that offers an opening to the secrets of birds. Perhaps Mom dreams of flying away with these birds, flying as high as a jet plane, flying far from the glass box that offers her shelter but little comfort. My heart breaks at the unspoken despair that might be sparking her quest. Can the Breakers be as menacing to her as it is to me? If that's the case, how can she stand to live here—a place she knows will be her final abode, a place she will never call home?

I can't know what my mother thinks, and I don't want to upset her by asking, but I keep digging into my own fears and come up with one probable answer. The Breakers threatens me because it makes the process of letting go be so comfortable, communal, inevitable, and banal. *This is where you will give up on life,* whispers every molecule of its filtered air. *This is the place where you come to die.*

We enter life screaming and gasping for breath, hungry for a mother's touch, the breast, the milk that sustains us. It irks me that so many of us will leave that life in a state of passivity, drugged with the inevitable if not with morphine. My mother understands her predicament and has chosen it. She knows she might end her hundred years in this alien yet comfortable place, surrounded by strangers or alone in her rooms—the television on with no one listening. But she is a fighter, and she will scream and gasp to her last breath, still hungry for life. Unlike my father whose creed it was, she will "not go gentle / into that good night."

I have been walking while I muse and am thrust back into the moment by Bruno. We have arrived at the wide beach past the breakwater at the Foster Avenue entrance. Bruno spots a flock of gulls standing one-legged at the edge of waves. I let him loose and he charges. The gulls wait until he is almost on them, rise in a wheeling mass, and land a few yards down the strand. He repeats his chase with the same result. After the third time, Bruno looks at me, bewildered. Nearby, a hooded, white-haired lady with a sack of bread crumbs laughs. I laugh with her and grab Bruno by the collar so he won't plunge into the lake after his mocking prey. This elderly woman throwing bread to gulls has recognized me as a version of herself. So do the women in the Breakers. Many are not older than I am and are in relatively good health. They smile as if I were a new neighbor. I smile back, but I'd like to believe I'm not like them.

Stop this rant, I tell myself. You have no right to feel holier than thou. Most of the dwellers in the Breakers have chosen to retire here. They have dreamed and saved to find safe harbor in a shiny glass building along the lake—a retreat where there will be no cooking and cleaning. No worries about property. No tedious, stressful jobs or family duties. In such a haven a person might relax, wear pretty clothes, enjoy a social life with peers, watch gulls dive into blue waters. If Mom wants intellectual stimulation, there are classes to take; if her wish is physical fitness, there's a pool and a gym, yoga and Pilates. Her doctor and her beauty shop are on the ground floor. Evenings she can go to in-house movies or musical events. Or ride the Breakers' bus with friends to shopping centers, symphony concerts, theaters.

When she was my age, my mother would have laughed at the idea of living in a retirement home. "No," she would have said. "No, no, no!" She and my father had slowed down but were still traveling, engaged in the lives they had lived, and self-sufficient. Now her husband is gone, her children live far away, and approaching one hundred, she needs help to get through each day. When we daughters suggest she should move to a retirement home in San Francisco, where she could be close to Carole and her family, where the weather is mild and life easier, she won't leave.

"This is where I live," she says. "I know the rules here. I know what to expect. I can't start again somewhere strange. Not anymore."

Like my mother, most of the people who reside at the Breakers are widows or widowers. They don't want to live with their progeny or be a burden to them. They have chosen limited independence and a community that offers solace if not hope. A recent widow will find new friends here. A widower might find romance. In this fine place, he tells himself, there will be *no more loneliness!*

Loneliness can be the greatest fear. It is not mine. At least not now. When I am no longer capable of driving, I believe I'll choose solitude on my mountain meadow. I will want a dog or two at my feet. And a caretaker to shop, cook, clean, and drive me to town to see family, friends, and doctors. Until my mind or hands or eyes no longer function, I will want a word processor, satellite television, and CDs playing my favorite music. There will be a stack of books by my armchair and a telephone at hand so I can talk to my children and grandchildren and surviving friends. Most days, I will sit near a window as I am doing now and look out at the sweep of grass and forest and cumulus clouds—pewter, pearl, dove gray. Like my mother, I will chart the courses of migrating hawks, of bluebirds and robins, and turkey vultures dipping on black wings over Bear Creek canyon. And I will drift into sleep as she does, feet up, head back, mouth open and gently snoring.

Dining In. The dining hall at the Breakers is a grand, light-filled room with a greenhouse-style curved glass roof and large windows looking out to the park. Even shut-ins who cannot stroll the lawns or be wheeled along its paths look out at apple blossoms in spring or the lush green foliage of summer as they spoon their bowls of oatmeal. Crunching bacon, they may watch winds blow yellow and red leaves in autumn. In winter, a mug of hot chocolate might warm their throats as a blizzard batters the panes.

Breakfast is casual, with diners helping themselves from a buffet laid out with melons, grapefruit, bananas, and prunes. It is common for breakfasters to sneak a couple of muffins into their purses, or a hard-boiled egg, or a banana for lunch, which is what my mother does. In her kitchenette I find stale muffins in the cupboard, rotting bananas on the counter. It gives her a *frisson* to get away with something for nothing, to be a little naughty. Like the thrill of shoplifting. My mother was caught lifting underpants on a group bus trip to Target. "You've got to keep a sharp eye on them," said the manager. The incident embarrassed Mom's caregiver, but not her.

In the buzzing dining room, people visit from one table to another. Breakfast is democratic, with no reserved seating, while dinner is a formal affair whose unspoken rules are as complex as the rituals in a high school cafeteria. Dinner is served from five to seven, and tables are set with white linens, menus, and cut flowers. The overcooked food will be served by immigrants in uniforms—only African Americans this visit, many newly arrived from Nigeria and Somalia. On my previous visit, the waiters were Hispanic. Color and ethnicity of the dining room staff changes with oft-changing administrators.

"Everyone has a clique," says Mom. This was the first thing she discovered about the Breakers. "And we dress up for dinner."

The cliques are hierarchical, running from North Shore suburbanites to the Near North elite. The most prestigious tables include a concert pianist, a nuclear physicist, and widows of CEOs. Mom points to a slim, well-coiffed woman in designer clothes. "We call her the Princess," she whispers. There are no princesses at Mom's table, only two sprightly Irish Catholic widows—one of whom is an avid Cubs fan and ushers at Wrigley Field during home games. Then there's a stout Polish woman who was a bureaucrat in the Democratic machine on Chicago's West Side, and Mother's new best friend, Victoria—a Jewish immigrant from Cairo via Paris.

"We eat with our group," Mother continues. "Always. We eat at the same time—six o'clock. I don't come down for lunch. I just grab a bite."

Standing in line for a table reservation, I feel like an anthropologist. It's easy to spot newcomers. They're the overdressed ones trying not to look out of it. A few loners sit by themselves by choice. Others sit alone because no one wants to be with them. And then there are the truly decrepit, still hanging on but destined for Assisted Living on the fourth floor. They sit in wheelchairs or slumped at a table with their caretakers lurking nearby. (Caretakers may not eat or sit in the dining room.)

Mother's dinner group used to consist of six women, but one moved to a nursing home and two died. Without much ado, the survivors added a new person. At the Breakers, people disappear. They go to the hospital and don't come back. Or they die in their beds, or trip on a rug, or are struck down while watching television.

Speaking of watching TV, "A strange thing happened last week," says Mom. "I woke up in the middle of the night. There was a noise. It was about two o'clock. I saw light coming from the living room. I knew I had shut off the TV. I always turn out the light. I thought I was going crazy."

Mom tiptoed down the hall and peeked into the living room. A man was sitting in her armchair, his back to her, and he was watching television, the sound turned up loud. She tiptoed back to the bathroom, locked the door, and pulled the emergency cord by the shower to alert the security guard in the lobby. She waited. No one came.

"I was desperate. I couldn't wait any longer." Mom touches her lips with her fingers in a shushing gesture. "So I tiptoed again down the hall and to the front door. He didn't hear me. I opened the door as quiet as a mouse. I ran to the elevator." She laughs. "I was in my nightgown. With bare feet."

As Mom rode down to the lobby, the security guard was on his way up to her apartment. It seems the guard had been taking a leak when she pulled the emergency cord. It seems he took a long one. I suspect he'd gone outside to smoke. Or maybe he was on a cell phone with his girlfriend. Hopefully, he wasn't sneaking a drink from a hidden bottle. By the time my mother returned to her apartment, the guard had a bewildered old fellow in a shoulder lock and was escorting him down to the lobby. The man was a neighbor from her floor who had lost his way. Either she had left her door unlocked or he was able to open it with his apartment's key. The man's relatives were called, and within a few days he was gone.

"I'm sorry for him," says Mom. "He was a nice man. Very quiet. He was confused. Not dangerous. He thought he was in his own house."

The implications of my mother's story frighten me. If the guard takes a break, who is watching for emergencies in a place where emergencies are the rule? I shudder to imagine what might happen if doors are so easily broached and help so slow to arrive. Mom shrugs. She is not alarmed. Maybe it's her Zoloft at work. She tells me there is a trip latch on every apartment's door, which is set by an attendant at night. It is released when the door is opened. If a resident's door remains unopened by ten the next morning, security is alerted. The guard knocks on the door and, if no one answers, he lets himself in. If necessary, he calls an ambulance. Which brings me to the death parade.

In this high-toned senior residence, news of death is accepted with an exclamation, or tears, if the departed was a friend, or a disinterested turn of the head. There is no wailing here. No tearing of hair. No one is supposed to see in public the sadness that gnaws at a person behind her mascara-black lashes and rouged cheeks. Each week, framed photos of the most recent deceased, along with embossed name cards and sometimes an obituary, are exhibited on a polished mahogany table in the lobby next to a vase of flowers. Residents check out that day's missing persons as if they were checking the weather report.

Habituated to loss, my mother has outlived most of the friends and relatives of her generation. She's got the constitution of a goat and the stubbornness of a donkey, but that doesn't stop Mom from paying her emotional dues. After my father died, she became depressed, losing some of the sparkle that defines her. She has been taking antidepressants ever since. Never stoic, she is stoic now. Perhaps this is due to chemicals inhibiting her brain's receptors. Perhaps it is caused by losses piling up until loss becomes the norm. Or, as some experts have found in recent studies, she may be one of many old people who become more content as they age, as long as they are not in pain and have no debilitating diseases. Stress drops away. There is no need to strive for the unreachable. A person knows her vulnerability and welcomes each good day. Acceptance of death must be part of this contentment—a consequence of living into old, old age.

Victoria. Mother's new best friend is Victoria. It's been a love match for both of them. Victoria is a French-speaking, poker-playing, ninety-year-old widowed Egyptian Jew of the merchant class. When, during World War II, fascists forced the Jews in the Cairo ghetto into exile, Victoria fled to Paris with her much older husband and two sons. After the war, they emigrated to Chicago and scraped together a new and eventually prosperous life.

Speaking French is what brought Mom and Victoria together. My mother loves everything French: the culture, the food, the clothes, the language. The best years of her life were the glittering Paris years of the 1920s and early '30s when she was a student at the Sorbonne, learned photography, became a successful young photographer for *Paris Vogue,* fell in love and got married, had a baby, and worked with my father in their own studio and apartment in Montparnasse.

Victoria speaks both French and English in a high-pitched, soft, almost babyish voice. Her hair is white and silky and page boy neat. Her bespectacled eyes are pale and blue, and she seems larger than she is, with legs and ankles swollen from heart failure and diabetes. Judging from her appearance, to say nothing of her pessimism and irony, she could easily be one of my Hungarian relatives. Lately, Victoria has taken to using a walker rather than her cane, but she retains her sense of elegance with blue and lavender silk dresses and hand-knit sweaters. The bib she ties around her neck at dinner sparkles silver.

After dinner, Victoria goes to the mezzanine to play poker with her card-shark pals. "You shouldn't bet against her," warns Mom. "She has tricks."

Poker is the one thing my mother cannot share with Victoria, although she too is a gambler, having played at sweepstakes for more than twenty years. Mother's mail consists largely of sweepstakes offers or news of prizes won. Her desk is piled with promises of instant wealth. We try to reason with her about the odds, but she is sure she will win big. "Then," she says, scrutinizing my face for new blemishes and wrinkles, "I will pay for you to have a face-lift."

While he was alive, Mom deferred to my father's increasing

isolation. Now, codependent no more, she can live the social life she once loved, but she is too picky to have many real friends. Victoria has been her key to joining the inner circles at the Breakers because Victoria is one of its earliest residents, and her friendship gives Mom status. More important, Victoria has become Mom's confidante, companion, and dinner partner. When we daughters come to visit, we take Mom and Victoria to an Arabian restaurant on Clark Street to feast on the Middle Eastern food that Victoria craves. They dress in their finest, toddle out of cabs with their walkers, eat couscous and shish kebab, and drink red wine. We bring lamb chops home in doggy bags—the luscious meat the old ladies love to order, which neither of them can chew.

"Oh, thank you," says Victoria, "it's so good to get away from that place." My sisters and I pray for Victoria's health. I shudder to imagine what will happen to Mom if Victoria turns up missing.

Esther. Before Victoria there was Esther. Esther Burns has been Mom's dearest friend for over half a century. A gracious, bright, and pretty woman who was first a labor organizer and then a high school history teacher, Esther has been struck by Alzheimer's. In her mid-eighties, she has a curvaceous figure; her turned-up nose is still perky; and she has quit dying her thin hair black, leaving it a silvery color. She still has enough long-term memory to reside in the land of the conscious and enough awareness to cause herself a great deal of anxiety. But Esther is in denial about the severity of her memory loss. Sometimes she joins Mom and Victoria at dinner. That is, when Esther remembers.

Only a few years ago, Esther and Mom hunted for bargains at T.J. Maxx and found treasures in suburban secondhand stores. They lunched and gossiped and planned trips together. No more. Lately, Mom tells me, Esther's children have hired a live-in Filipina woman to give her daily medications, to dress her, to accompany her when she goes out, and even to sleep in the same bed with her. Each month one of her sons comes to visit from the Bay Area, or her daughter arrives from New York. This is a relief for my mother, who feels responsible for Esther being here.

Mom enticed Esther to move to the Breakers after her husband, Ben, died. Since then, Esther's loss of mind has gotten steadily worse, but our mother has not been willing or able to act as her caretaker. Being a caretaker and homemaker was Mom's vocation after she gave up her photographic partnership with my father, but these days it's all she can do to care for herself.

"I called her this morning to say you were here," says Mom, "but she was not in. I left a message. She will forget as soon as she puts down the phone."

"Maybe we'll see her at breakfast."

Mother sniffs. "With her crazy friends. You know, I think she has a boyfriend . . ."

"Good," I say, smiling at Mom's jealousy. "I'm delighted Esther's found some new friends."

As luck will have it, Esther is walking toward the elevators as we step out. "Annick!" she cries. She has not forgotten my face or name. "Such a surprise. How long are you staying?"

I give her a hug. "I'm taking Mom to Sawyer."

"Sawyer," she says. "Can I go with you?"

Mom looks at me and shakes her head. Esther's cottage on Lake Michigan is located down the road from ours. She and Ben had followed us there in the 1940s, buying the poet Carl Sandburg's lakeside studio. And when we moved to Wilmette in the fifties, they soon bought a house nearby. The Burns were the closest friends our family had—like an uncle and aunt to me and my sisters—and their daughter and two sons are as dear to us as cousins.

Ben Burns had started his career as a radical journalist and editor for Chicago's left-wing papers. Then he worked for years as one of the founders and the managing editor of *Ebony* magazine, until it was no longer cool for a white person to edit a black magazine. He and my father had become friends before World War II as compatriots in Chicago's far-left political movement—actually the Communist Party—which I believe also included Studs Terkel and Nelson Algren. Those renegade artists and writers remained friends long after they were kicked out of the party for refusing to adhere to the Stalinist line. It was a blessing for me to grow up in their midst. A blessing and an example.

When he grew older, Ben would become a successful public relations guy as well as an editor, and his politics would become more conservative, but during his *Ebony* days, he often commissioned my father to take photos for feature stories, including black-and-white portraits of black celebrities. Once, when Kathy was ten and I was twelve, we came to the Deutch Studio on Wacker Drive after ballet lessons. And there was Duke Ellington sitting on an Eames chair in front of a wall-sized collage my father had made of a classical Greek statue. I see that studio in vivid detail: the glass-brick room divider that separated the office from the dressing room, the darkroom with its red light, the side office where Mom did the fine work of retouching, and the huge open studio with tall spotlights, ladders, white backdrops, and the oversize camera my father used to take pictures.

The day we met Ellington, my father was sitting behind his Danish Modern desk smoking a cigarette. The Duke was spiffy in a hipster hat, and he sported a small mustache. I remember his bulk and the smell of manly perfume. He rose from his seat when my father introduced us. Then he kissed us both hard on the lips!

During Ben's and Dad's *Ebony* years we met Lena Horne but not Mahalia Jackson, whom I revered and whose portrait Daddy also took, and sadly not Joe Lewis, whom I would have been awed to meet in person. But I did meet Jackie Robinson. And the most prized childhood picture I own features me and Jackie at Wrigley Field the year Robinson joined the Brooklyn Dodgers. I was eleven. In the published photo my father shot I hold a baseball for Robinson to sign and wear a beret with green ribbons (Mom's idea of what an American girl should wear to a ballgame). My French braids fall to my waist. The black teenage boy who stands next to me is more hip, with a felt hat and safari jacket.

Ben and Esther were an exceptionally close couple, and after Ben died, Esther became inconsolable. Bringing her with us to Sawyer today would be a full-time job. Still, it is hard for me to say no to Esther. She is as attached to Sawyer as my mother is. It is their hearth place, the location of memory and solace where they raised their kids, entertained their grandkids, and lived with their husbands through youth and old age. Those beach cottages in the dunes are the only places she and my mother call home. It breaks Esther's heart to be left behind; and it breaks mine to have to hurt her.

Esther has coffee with us. My mother is nearly deaf, and even with hi-tech hearing aids, it is hard for her to understand talk around a table. Eating is one of her remaining pleasures, and breakfast is her favorite meal. She carefully spreads cream cheese on her muffins. Picks at her cantaloupe. She looks up at me with a sly smile. Deafness has advantages. The most precious is being able to tune out any conversation that disturbs or bores her.

"How are the boys?" asks Esther. She repeats this question five times, no matter how I respond. "My kids are coming to take me to Sawyer," she says. She frowns. "I'm not sure when. What day is it today?"

"May 13." Esther writes the date in a little notebook in her purse. "Excuse me a minute," she says. "I've got to go upstairs and call Bobbie. She'll know."

When Esther returns, she has changed from a red silk blouse to a bright blue patterned one. "You look nice," I say. "That's a pretty blouse."

"What are the boys doing? When are you going to Sawyer?"

"Did you reach Bobbie?"

"She wasn't there." Esther smiles nervously. "I forget what I wanted to ask her."

"Come up to Mom's place," I suggest. "I've got my dog up there. I'd like you to meet him." Dog? Esther looks puzzled. Sure enough, in a few minutes, she is at the door. I introduce Esther to Bruno, thinking this teddy-bear creature will be a comfort, but she ignores him. All she can think of is Sawyer. Her son Steve told me that the last time he'd taken her there, they stayed for a week. Then, driving back to Chicago, she asked him, "Please, Stevie, . . . let's go to Sawyer."

Esther looks at me with a sadness so deep I almost fall into it. "Damn Ben for dying on me! It wasn't supposed to be like this."

HOUSE IN
THE DUNES

DAYS FOUR AND FIVE,
MAY 14–15

Outer Drive. I take the Outer Drive along the lakeshore's pale green parkways, which this damp morning are flecked yellow, pink, and violet with daffodils and apple blossoms and beds of wide-eyed pansies. Sailboats and yachts are moored in Belmont Harbor, and a few white sails wing across the lake.

This ride is so familiar I could dream every turn and name every landmark. We pass the lagoon at the borders of the Lincoln Park Zoo, where my father took us for rowboat rides on warm Sunday afternoons. On the other side of the zoo is Francis Parker School, where I was lucky to spend fourth through eighth grades. The school was and still is a progressive institution, and it infused me with intellectual ardor and moral awareness, but the Victorian manor where we studied and played has long since been replaced by a modern structure, and with it my sense of belonging.

The Outer Drive's southern stretch leads past an even more personal neighborhood. Here are the University of Chicago streets where I walked as a bride at nineteen and pushed Eric's buggy as a twenty-year-old mother. It is tempting to let nostalgia take over, but I am getting bored with my self-obsessed vision. We turn inland at the Museum of Science and Industry, wind through Washington Park, and pass into the black ghetto at Stony Island Avenue, ascending over it on the Chicago Skyway.

Bruno sits in the back of the SUV, head up, looking out the partly open rear window and sniffing new territories. His two hundred million ethmoidal or olfactory cells read the world in precise degrees of scent, as opposed to my fifty million, which are not enough to divert me from reading the world through my eyes. According to German canine scientist Walter Neuhaus, a dog's nose is from one million to one hundred million times more sensitive to smell than mine is. Bruno smells the environment more intensely than he sees it, but contrary to popular assumptions, he is not color-blind. Like all dogs, Bruno sees muted colors— indistinct greens, yellows, purples, shades of gray—which, I realize, is how I am seeing my past today.

I pull onto the Indiana Toll Road against Mom's objections. Her reluctance is a hangover inherited from my father, whose Depression mind-set would not allow him to pay a toll if he could drive for free. He would detour miles out of the way to stop at his favorite gas station, which offered the cheapest gas and low-priced cartons of Kent cigarettes.

My detour veers toward comfort. I hate the truck traffic on Interstate 94. The $2.50 it costs to ride the toll road is worth every penny. We take the Lake Station exit, leaving the industrial ruins of Gary behind and joining I-94 East. The landscape morphs into fields of young grass on either side of the road. Low hills are feathered with new-leaved trees. Eighty miles separate Chicago from our cottage in the dunes. Worlds so close, and yet we have entered a different country.

Red Arrow. We escape the freeway at New Buffalo and turn north on the Red Arrow Highway, which borders Lake Michigan's shores. When I was a child and there was no freeway, my father would slow down as we neared Union Pier, lean back in his black Buick, and light a Chesterfield. I loved that first whiff of smoke just as I loved the acrid odor of freshly pumped gas and associate both with loving my father. My little sisters and I would lift our heads from our books or stop our word games to check out the familiar fruit stands and antique shops. Daddy always stopped at the Swedish bakery in Harbert, where Mom would buy a loaf of anise-spiced Swedish rye bread, a raspberry coffee cake, and a dozen coconut macaroons while we begged for cream-filled chocolate doughnuts.

Red Arrow. I used to mull over the name, imagining we were speeding toward the wild woods where Indians lived in tepees and bears roamed with elk and wolves as they had a century earlier. Sixty years later I still get a tremor of anticipation when we roll onto the Red Arrow Highway. Mom has been dozing but perks up at the turn. "Let's stop for a hamburger," she says, meaning we must have our ritual lunch at Redamak's—a great barn of a joint where burgers are served on a doily that is also a menu. Mom picks a booth at a window. She sits across from me, her chin just above table level, peeling off pieces of bun and taking small bites from her cheeseburger.

"At the Breakers, they don't know how to make a hamburger," she says. "They don't know nothing. I have to force myself to eat that food." She wipes grease from her lips and offers me half of her glass of brown beer.

Simple familiar pleasures such as burgers and beer are what Mom and I are after. We have entered the country of beech forests, moving dunes, and blue waters—the place of *vacation* for me and my family, and for Esther left behind—*vacate* being the operative notion, not *vacant*. As we approach the stone stanchions that mark the entrance to our road in Tower Hill Shorelands, Mom begins to sing in her quivery, off-key voice, "Sawyer, Sawyer, here we come," echoing the tune we girls used to sing as we drew near to our cottage. I pitch in for old times' sake.

Since my last trip, the gravel road has been improved. There are a couple of new houses on the forested hills. And along the urine-tinted creek where we used to trap tadpoles in glass jars is a three-story blue residence with a kite calling welcome. Still, the community has retained its rustic isolation—qualities necessary for the spiritual retreat it was meant to be, reserved for Congregational ministers and their families.

"Tell me again how you and Daddy found this place," I ask Mom. "No way were you two Congregational."

"You are forgetting about your sisters."

Mom flashes her wicked smile. Shortly after we moved from Chicago to Wilmette in 1950, Kathy (eleven years old) was recruited by her new best friend, the daughter of the Congregational minister, to join their church. Soon she brought six-year-old Carole into the fold. My agnostic, upwardly mobile immigrant parents were experts at assimilation and accepted their daughters' conversions with irony. They knew being Protestant was a chance for the girls to become accepted in this white wealthy suburb where we were rumored to be the first Jewish family. And they knew it wouldn't last forever.

Predictably, my sisters' churchgoing did not extend beyond high school. And I, although feeling the need and the pull, could never get myself to join any formal religious institution. At fourteen, I was a friendless freshman in a big new high school where most kids had grown up with each other and fit into predetermined cliques. Desperate for connection, I believed the hole in my life could be filled by religion. I studied passages from the Old Testament and the New, checked out Buddhism in the *Encyclopaedia Britannica*, and found myself attracted to animistic American Indian religions. I went to Catholic mass, Protestant churches, and the Bahá'í temple in Evanston that was shaped like a giant white orange squeezer. I found beauty and wisdom in religious texts and rituals, but none could change my skeptical mind or touch my heart. I was Jewish by culture but not by faith and could find no spiritual sanctuary outside of a kind of idiosyncratic nature worship.

"We used to go to Lakeside when you were little," says Mom, breaking my reverie, "but that is where you caught the polio. We did not feel safe there anymore. So we looked for other places."

In 1943 a realtor took her and my father to see a boarded-up cottage overlooking the lake at Tower Hill Shorelands. It was finished on the outside, raw on the inside. My parents wanted to buy it right away, but the owner told my father it would take a while because there was a gentlemen's agreement among the property owners that required unanimous permission before any lot could be sold.

"No, thank you," said my father. "I'm not interested in a place where everyone is not accepted." Daddy was an ex-Communist immigrant Jew. He would have no truck with gentlemen's agreements.

"Mr. Mitchell came to the studio," says Mom. "He said we would be approved. No question. I begged your daddy, but he wouldn't listen."

That spring they kept looking for property but found nothing comparable, and by summer's end Mom had persuaded my father to take a second look. What Mom wants, she usually gets. She is the most tenacious person I've known, and her stubbornness can drive me to pound walls or chain-smoke or run into the street in a fury. Or laugh. It's one reason why Dave and I escaped to Seattle after Eric was born and Dave finished law school.

Mom adored her first grandchild—a boy after a generation of girls. She knew how to care for a baby and loved nothing better. At twenty I was unsure of my mothering qualities and afraid Mom would take over my son, which she was more than willing to do. Dave had grown up fatherless and independent of parental authority. He could not accept my parents' interference—especially my father's financial aid and the emotional strings attached. Competition between Dave and my father had begun while we were courting and accelerated after we married. Separation seemed the only way to keep the battle for dominance at bay.

I agreed it was necessary to flee. We chose Seattle—as far as we could run from Chicago. And then Montana, even farther away, in spirit as well as topography.

Mom continues her Sawyer story. "We saw a mixed couple and their children eating ice-cream cones at the Beach House," she says. "I thought that was promising." Then they learned that Carl Sandburg lived at Tower Hill, as did Louis Gottschalk, a well-known professor of French literature at the University of Chicago, and his Russian wife, Fruma. These were intellectuals they could identify with. So for $5,000 my parents bought the lot on the wooded dune, the unfinished house, and a private stretch of beach. They paid an additional $4,000 for an architect, a well, landscaping, and furnishings.

Kathy and I spent the next summers in a chaos of lumber, sawdust, and sand, playing on the beach while Carole learned to walk and to dog-paddle in her inner tube. We practiced synchronized water ballet, collected fossils called Indian stones, did cartwheels on the sand, and played Monopoly with the Gottschalk boys while carpenters put up knotty pine walls in the living and dining rooms, laid floors over the open joists of the front porch, and spread new linoleum in the kitchen.

Sixty years later, we're still at it—painting, digging a new foundation, repairing ancient plumbing. Playing house. The Tower Hill community has a homeowners' association but no more gentlemen's agreements. Because almost every bit of lakefront from the Indiana dunes to northern Michigan has been bought for summer homes, property values have shot so high that no struggling artists like my parents can afford to buy in, yet our retreat remains rustic. Maples, oaks, beeches, and pines still blanket the hills, and the dunes and beaches running north are protected from development by Warren Dunes State Park, which stretches more than three miles along the shore. Crisscrossed by trails and pocked with parking lots, the park is no wilderness. But it was my wilderness as a child—a preserve for deer, fox, wild turkey, and a host of native flora and fauna.

South of our place the blowouts and dunes have been bull-dozed for subdivisions. McMansions are displacing cottages in narrow lots on sandy bluffs. When we walk along the beach, my sisters and I sometimes hold our left hands up to shield our eyes from this carnage. But we walk with the pride of ownership, for in 1996, when Dad's health took a nosedive, he and Mom deeded the cottage to us. Now Kathy and Carole and I are sitting on a gold mine. Our two-story white frame home—more exactly, the property it sits on—is worth more than a million dollars. If we decide to sell, we will have to pay capital gains taxes, but the profits could underwrite nursing homes or home care or catastrophic illnesses, which become more likely as old age creeps up.

Happy to say, Sawyer was and still is the gathering place for us and for the eight children we spawned. When they were young, our kids would arrive in July from Boston, Montana, and San Francisco and stay a couple of weeks or a month under the abundant care of their grandparents. We mommies (divorced, widowed, or both) would join them—at least for a week or two.

The cousins played softball, made superhero Super 8 movies, dunked one another, and bonded forever. Now most have kids of their own. Soon they will inherit their mothers' shares and will have to decide whether to keep Sawyer or sell it or buy each other out. I'm glad I will not be involved in what is sure to be a struggle among cousins who need cash and cousins who need continuity; between those with children and those without; or those who treasure the place for its family connections and those who have places they treasure more.

Property can fracture families. Hopefully, Sawyer will remain a force for cohesion—the initiation ground for a new generation of children who will learn to dive under each other's legs and build castles in the sand.

Bruno's Heaven. I lug two armloads of groceries from the car and up the long stairway to the top of the dune where our cottage sits. Free at last, Bruno stops to consider the landscape. I wonder if he will balk because of his stairway phobia and run through the woods, coating his feet, belly, and sides with the poisonous oils of poison ivy. But he is not phobic about stairs without slats. "Good boy," I say, holding on to Mother's arm when Brunie charges past.

Bruno stands at the top landing, king of the mountain. He curls his lip into a lopsided smirk. Nose to the ground, he circles the house. Scents of squirrels, raccoons, mice, and other small critters have transported him into dog ecstasy. His tail wags nonstop. When I unlock the door to the kitchen, he dashes in. I chase after him, afraid he will crash into one of my father's sculptures or run over my tiny mother, but when I get to her she is patting Bruno's big head.

"I love this dog," says Mom, repeating her Bruno mantra. He makes a couple of grunting noises and settles at her feet—actually *on* her foot. No doubt about it, this dog knows our trip ends here. After stowing our groceries, I take Bruno for his first beach walk. He plows down the peeling green-painted stairs, crosses the little bridge across a gully, stops on the sandy path, looks back at me for permission. "Go ahead," I tell him, stepping out of my flip-flops. "You can go."

We are both running in the fine cool sand through clumps of knife-sharp marram grass and between flowering chokecherry brush till we reach the mini-dune that leads to the beach. This year our strip of waterfront sand is wide and flat. Some years it is narrow. Some years, sloping. The dunes move, and the beach moves. Wind makes a difference. Also rainfall and snow and the rising and falling of lake levels.

Brunie races in circles, jumps up at me, and licks my face. He hops around in his brown-dog dance. This is joy. This is gratitude. The lake is choppy and wavelets are cold on my toes. Bruno wades in until his feet lose touch with the bottom. He paddles a dozen yards, huffing as he does when swimming, then circles back. He shakes water off his back, finds a stick of driftwood, and drops it at my feet. I throw the stick and he plunges after it. I walk down the beach and he follows, head up, stick in jaws, tail and rear end wagging. I toss the stick again and again, and he retrieves it until he gets as bored as I am.

I look up toward the house, knowing my mother is sitting in her favorite wicker rocker on the screened porch, and then I hear the bell. How many times have I been called by that cowbell to leave some beachly pleasure and attend to hanging laundry or packing groceries up the stairs, helping with dinner or getting ready for bed? We kids used to hide from our grandmother Serene—a woman rarely, if ever, serene—who tugged at the bell rope, madly summoning us to lunch. If my mother was the bell ringer, we'd ignore her until she came stalking down the stairs to collar us.

I smile to myself. This is the way my boys have treated me. I whistle for Bruno. He is no model of obedience but better at the practice than me or my kin. The sun is low. The bell rings. The wheel turns.

Father's Ashes. I wake in the early morning, my bladder screaming. Bruno snores on his dog bed, but there will be no more sleep for me. Tiptoeing down the carpeted stairs to the dawn-dim living room, I am confronted by my father's gaunt, Brillo-haired ghost. It sits on the chairs he sat on, prowls the screened porch. The very air rising from the lake seems to carry a wisp of his tobacco breath.

Most immediately, my father's ghost resides in his sculptures. On a glass shelf next to our nonfunctional brick fireplace is the kneeling archer he carved in 1920s Paris. It is small and finely wrought, like a figure on a Grecian urn, more delicate than any carving my father was able to fashion with his arthritic joints after he retired from photography at age seventy-five. In Paris, young Pista created accordion players, tightrope walkers, hefty nudes, ballet dancers. His hands were nimble, and, infatuated with the human body, he became obsessed with depicting in hardwood the qualities of grace.

Fifty years later, his vision had become blatantly sexual or purely abstract, and most of his sculptures were filled with pain and sorrow, as he was. His large strong hands had grown coarse from darkroom chemicals. Twisted with age, they lost the finesse needed for detail. Arthritis stiffened every joint—especially his worn-out right shoulder. No matter. Daddy set up his workbench in the kitchen alcove where windows look out to the lake on one side and the woods on the other. He is alive there in my memory—a bony old man on a high stool watching for cardinals and blue jays between bouts of carving. Scraps and curls of fragrant cherry wood collect under his feet. He is making a whale.

As I pass the low cabinet by the downstairs bath, I touch the swelling belly of the completed whale mother; her baby swims below her, attached by a thin pole. I walk toward sliding glass doors that open onto the porch. A dolphin floats head down as if diving toward the lake. This is one of my father's late, rare, lighthearted figures. Meanwhile, on the slatted coffee table by the daybeds a ring of naked tribal women dance around a giant erect penis. Perhaps this sculpture is my father's idea of a joke. Perhaps not. I, however, will never welcome it into *my* living room.

Bruno pads down the stairs and trails after me as I turn toward the dining area. We pass a starving man on a pedestal. He is African in body, universal in spirit, and holds the washrag body of his dead child in outstretched arms. Bruno whines softly. I whisper, "Hold on, big fellow," not sure why I am whispering or why I don't feel like letting him out to pee.

Off to our right, behind the varnished picnic table where the family gathers for meals, is a larger sculpture silhouetted against

French doors looking out to the flagstone terrace. This hunk of rough-hewn wood still shaggy with bark sits like a tree stump on its three-legged stool. Faces peer out on all sides: a weeping woman with long hair; a man open-mouthed, screaming. Some of the faces are beautiful, others hideous. All are suffering. I return to the kitchen to make a pot of strong coffee. Bruno looks up at me and nudges my knee. He is hungry and has to relieve himself. "Just a minute," I tell him. "I'm busy."

In the alcove where my father's heavy workbench stood, we have placed a knotty pine breakfast table and a couple of barstools. When she wakes and finishes her hour-long toilette, Mom will perch here. She will look for birds at the feeder that mostly feeds fat squirrels. She will sip her decaf coffee and eat her heated coffee cake. She will pay no notice to the skeletal figure that stands on the table a couple of feet to her left. This was my father's last, unfinished work. The wood is pale and raw. The old man has thin bowed legs like my father's and a faceless head encased in a cowl. Maybe it is a self-portrait. Maybe death itself.

Bruno whimpers. There can be no more putting him off. I let him out, confident he will come back soon to be fed. The sun is up and I am still lost in thoughts of my father. I wish my memories of the vital Steve Deutch whom I adored when I was a girl were as vivid as my memories of the old man who carved that death's-head figure. Although all of us embody many personas from childhood through maturity and any one of them is as real as any other, if we survive to old age, it seems the final feeble, demented creature will be the one embedded in memory.

Photos are no cure. Images of my young father with his tightly muscled torso and aquiline profile are like movie posters—distant and idealized. He throws a softball to a pigtailed daughter (me) on the beach. My little sister Kathy rides horsey on his shoulders. A group photo on the terrace shows him with his brother Gene, both dark and short-waisted in tight white T-shirts, good looking in a middle-European way; and around them are strung us six girl cousins arranged by height.

At twelve, I am the tallest, coy and hormonal in my off-the-shoulder peasant blouse. Kathy stands next to me. She is slim and flirty, with a pageboy haircut framing her heart-shaped face. Carole, at five, in pinafore and curls, is last in line after our stair-step cousins Nancy, Susie, and Margie. Carole holds our dachshund, Schnitzel. My father's parents sit on lawn chairs. Grandma Deutch is round and owlish, with no noticeable neck and round glasses. Grandpa is lean and severe. I think of a nursery rhyme— *Jack Sprat could eat no fat. His wife could eat no lean.* Grandma Beck smiles sedately. Her pretty face sags with the gravity of years. These grandparents are not much older than I am now, yet in my mind they are old in a way I can never be. Mom is missing because she is the one taking the picture.

My father had been the rooster in our henhouse. Macho and strong, he was in command of himself (if not always us) throughout his working life and into retirement. Then old age betrayed him. His body became atrophied and pained with arthritis and sciatica, he wheezed and coughed with emphysema, but it was his mind that cut him down. By his mid-eighties my Dad was too forgetful and confused to be trusted with driving. He endangered my mother, his daughters, grandchildren, and strangers on the highways and streets where he found himself lost. But he was in denial. "You're a menace," we told him, together and in turn. "You will kill Mom."

"You want to take away my independence," he countered. "For you, I am not a man anymore. Just a burden." He thought losing his wheels was equivalent to losing his manhood, but there were more indignities to come. My father tripped on the living room rug in Chicago, breaking his hip. After surgery, he was incarcerated for rehabilitation in a nursing home he dreaded and despised. And when he came home he had to use a walker or be transported with a wheelchair. Still worse, he began to be tormented by hallucinations and brain seizures. Now he had to rely on his daughters and grandchildren to bring him and my mother to Sawyer.

But even in those last hard years, being at the lake could bring on a smile, a tender kiss, a sigh of contentment. I see my father in the slanting light of late afternoon dozing on the cottage's screened porch, feet up in his wicker chaise longue. *Time* magazine, which he reads religiously, lies open in his lap. Or he is in his straight-backed armchair in the living room, backlit in rosy hues from the setting sun. His iron-gray hair sticks out behind his ears like mine tends to do. He is watching the "MacNeil/Lehrer NewsHour," a shot of Scotch whiskey in his hand. My father turns to me and his eyes are keen, no sign of dementia right now. He is as opinionated as ever. We talk the familiar talk of politics.

When he was younger, my father was a man in constant motion. He'd be fixing something damaged, digging, pruning, cleaning, or whittling at his sculptures—finding something to occupy his hands. A perfectionist, he made me feel guilty about being a slacker, or made me be mad about feeling guilty. Even in old age, so stove-up he could barely move, Daddy insisted on raking autumn leaves at the cottage, shoving great swaths down the hill. He tripped on a fallen branch, tumbled after the leaves, emerged bruised but not broken. It pleased him to burn piles of dead leaves at the bottom of the hill as he had burned fallen leaves outside our house in Wilmette. Burning is illegal now, but what did he care? The last time he tried, he set the woods on fire and we had to call the fire department.

Father's ashes are buried above the flagstone terrace and stone wall he laid by hand almost sixty years ago, throwing his back out in the process. They lie under lilies of the valley and red columbine near the ancient oak where Bruno is lifting his leg. Sixty years is a long time, even for an already mature oak, and like me and my parents, it has become gnarled and broken. When we were kids, my sisters and I used to ride a swing made of thick ropes and a wooden seat, which Daddy hung from the tree's overhanging arm (now amputated). We pumped our legs over the edge of our hilltop toward the lake's endless waters and returned with our feet as high as we could get them, trying to touch the branch's low-hanging sun-tipped leaves.

On a June day in 1997, I stood across from that gnarled oak with Mom and Kathy. We were trying to find a level place in which to bury our father's ashes. I dug a hole in the pale gray, sandy earth. Kathy, annoyingly thinner, more feminine and emotional, was near to tears. Mom bent her head. We must have made a strange picture: the tiny, hunched old woman flanked by her age-defying daughters wearing shorts and halters, their curling white and gray hair falling across bare shoulders. Daddy's bemused ghost peered down at us, letting out a sound between a laugh and a sob. It is hard to know what Mom felt. She remained unnaturally impassive. The three of us took turns tipping his ashes into the hole. When it was my time, I let the ashes run through my fingers, startled that Daddy's remains were gritty, intermingled with bits of bone, more coarse and lumpy than I had imagined.

The yellowish stream poured into the hole and became part of the dune. Kat and I took turns reciting our father's favorite poems by Dylan Thomas (*Do not go gentle into that good night*) and Richard Hugo (*I'll leave believing we keep all we lose and love*), and then we planted a little pine over his grave to be his living monument. By spring the pine tree was dead. Perhaps it froze that winter. Or no one was there to water it. Or my father's ashes were so toxic they burned the tree's tender roots.

That summer we planted a second pine—a native that should have survived—and it died too. So we gave up. Now a hunk of granite marks Dad's spot. It was chosen by Carole, who was not present at the burial of ashes. Carole has coarse white hair cut short as a boy's and a prominent arched nose inherited from the father whose perfectionism and assertive nature she has taken as her own. She found the perfect stone. It is uneven and striated in grays, about a foot and a half long, with curves and a fluid heft that reminds us of our father's sculptures. His name is etched into it. Dates of birth and death: *Stephen Deutch (Pista) 1907–1997.* No other words.

Mother's Ashes. Mom helped Carole choose our father's gravestone, and as they drove back to the cottage Carole said, "Have you thought about what you want us to do with *your* ashes?"

Daddy, typically anal, had typed out detailed instructions about how we should handle his remains and belongings. Mom did not like to ponder such matters.

"She was quiet . . . thoughtful," says Carole. "Then I asked if she wanted her ashes to be buried alongside Dad's."

"No," Mom said, without hesitation.

"She didn't explain. I didn't ask."

A minute passed in silence. "Throw them into the lake," said Mom. After another silent stretch, she finished her thought. "You never know what will happen to the house. But the lake will be there forever."

My alternate memory of our mother's wishes comes from a conversation we had on the porch in Sawyer during the dusky moments after sunset. In Carole's memory, our mother is thoughtful and philosophical. In mine she is angry. Memories are like that. As the neuroscientist Oliver Sacks has eloquently explained, we make up stories from actual incidents that validate our notions of who we are and explain our connections to a past history that we have also imagined—at least in part.

Like Carole, I ask my mother if she wants her ashes buried next to our father's. Her answer is the same. "No. I want you to throw my ashes in the lake."

"Why?" I ask the leading question. "Are you still so angry at him?"

"Yes. He hurt me too much."

Mom is referring to my father's infidelities, an easy vice for a woman-loving photographer surrounded by models. She does not mean his one-night stands, which she dismisses like a French wife, with a metaphoric wink.

"Maybe he cheated sometimes," she says. "That was not important. To me he was a lover." She smiles a bit wickedly. "You know . . . your Daddy. When he came for the weekend (he worked in the city during the week), he couldn't wait for you children to go to sleep. He wanted to make love to me all the time."

What hurt her to the point of no forgiveness are two serious betrayals. The first hit while my father's older brother Gene was in a hospital suffering the final stages of liver cancer. Dad's oldest brother, Alfred, had committed suicide in Chicago in 1931 at age twenty-nine. Now Gene was dying at fifty-five and my father was distraught. Night after night he sat at Gene's bedside. He watched him die.

Daddy had just passed fifty. He had always been vulnerable and emotional in the extreme, but now he was in the throes of a midlife crisis. His daughters had flown the nest—me to Seattle, Kathy to San Francisco, and Carole was finishing high school and about to go to France for a year. His photography business was commercially successful but not artistically exciting, and his wife of more than twenty-five years had settled into suburban middle age. My father believed his life was in decline, yet he was still vital. Where had his youthful dreams of art and creativity fled? What could he look forward to that was not predictable? So he did what many men and women do in similar situations. He fell in love. Furious and passionate love with Gene's blonde assistant, Zee—a young southern woman who was nothing like my mother.

I never asked my father how or why he chose this unlikely woman to be the catalyst that would recharge his life. And I'm sure he would have given me no answer, even if he thought he had one. So I have made up a story that fits my sense of him. Forgive this amateur psychological guess, but I believe my father was trying to keep his brother magically alive by appropriating his carefree way of life. Including the attractive young southerner who was Gene's assistant.

"Wait," my father begged Mom. "I know this won't last. Wait and I'll come back to you. I promise."

Mom was unable to wait. Not then. Not ever. She imagined every night what was going on in another woman's bed. "Me or her," she said.

Driven by passion, my father chose his lover, breaking my mother's already broken heart. They divorced, and Dad married Zee, giving Mom the house and alimony and child support. Mom held on until Carole graduated from New Trier, then sold the house in Wilmette. It must have been a bitter leaving. The stucco three-story on Greenwood was where she'd enjoyed a ten-year fifties idyll—mothering her girls, decorating, learning to sew, gardening, cooking gourmet meals, hosting coffee klatches, and playing bridge with ladies of the neighborhood. But her dream ended in betrayal, so she moved back to the familiar city with her mother, renting an apartment on Chicago's Near North Side and taking a job selling art at Marshall Fields. Gray-haired, divorced, and in her mid-fifties, Mom began to build a new life.

Meanwhile, my father's marriage to Zee predictably ship-wrecked. Like Professor Henry Higgins in *My Fair Lady*, he had tried to transform a sexy Georgia girl into a sophisticated woman of culture. But Zee was no child like the daughters whose educations and aspirations he had shaped, and despite art lessons and concerts and a new wardrobe, the transformation did not take. I can't blame Zee for being resentful. At loose ends in Deerfield, with no kids, no work, questionable self-esteem, and a guilt-plagued older husband, Zee must have been bored and unhappy. She took to bedding a local policeman who had been a lover. Surprising them together, Dad slapped Zee in a rage, then filed for divorce.

That December, after the divorce was final, he called us in Montana to wish our family Merry Christmas. Mom was visiting for the holidays. "Ask your mother if she will talk to me," said Daddy. "I have something important to tell her."

Hesitant, but urged on by me, Mom took the phone. I retreated to the kitchen. They talked for a long time and when she hung up, Mom's face was flushed. Her eyes filled with tears. "He wants to see me again." She blew her nose. "I don't know if I can bear it."

Mom went to her room and slammed the door. She stayed in bed for two days. I was worried, handing chicken broth and tea on a tray through the door as if she'd been struck by the flu. I tried to talk with her but she shooed me away. Not even her grandsons were able to tease her out of hiding. When Mom emerged, she was her usual cheerful self. It was a glorious, sunny winter's day, with a foot of new-fallen snow. She took Eric and Stevie sledding down Lolo Street in the Flyer sleds she had given them for Christmas. "We'll see," she said.

It was hard for Mom to gag down her considerable pride and allow her ex-husband to woo her. But that's what Dad did, dating his ex-wife of twenty-five years, convincing her this time the union would be equal, that he would take her to see the world, and they would do the things they had always planned to do. But most important was bringing cohesion back to the family circle. Family was the connection my parents prized above all things— a past and a present and a future that only they could properly share.

In the spring they remarried—strangely, on May 11, 1965, my twenty-ninth birthday, and eighteen days before Kathy's New York wedding. We daughters were not invited. My father's best friend, Nelson Algren, was their witness. It was a civil ceremony at the Cook County Courthouse, and afterward the friends celebrated with retsina and lamb kebabs and cakes running with honey at their favorite restaurant in Greektown.

For the next twenty years, my mother traveled the world with my father, as promised—Turkey and France, Hungary and Poland, Egypt and the Sahara and Mali and India. They winterized the house in Sawyer and spent peaceful years and months in their haven. Dad retired from his photography business at age seventy-five, finally able to devote what energies he had to his first and most beloved art—sculpting. And then came the bad last years when my father became chronically ill, in pain, reclusive, and delusional. Mom took care of him to the end, suffering the abuse he threw at her with no complaint—part of the bargain she'd made when they remarried.

Generosity is one thing, but forgiveness is tougher. Since his death, Mom has had years as a widow to pick at her scars, and what she cannot forgive is his last betrayal—a clandestine but, he swore, unconsummated affair with a teenage Korean girl whom they had taken in as a boarder while she went to high school. Shades of Woody Allen!

"I want to throw up when I think about it," says Mom. "He makes me sick. He could be her grandfather—an old man more than seventy years old! I don't blame her. She was young. What did she know? But he should know better . . ." She sighs and shakes her head. "I was blind. They were kissing and holding hands in my house! How could he do such a thing?"

One of my regrets is that while our mother was like the proverbial three monkeys who see no evil, hear no evil, speak no evil, I was suspicious. On one visit to Chicago when the moon-faced Korean girl must have been sixteen or seventeen, the perfume of pheromones was so heavy in my parents' apartment I almost smelled the sexual messages flowing between her and my father. Recognition came easily because when I was pubescent and rife with hormones I had to deal with my attraction to and rejection of my father's love—at least its physical manifestations. He never molested me, but his hugs and kisses were too intense, too sexual. He would take my face in both hands and look into my eyes, and then he'd kiss me on the mouth. I'm sure he didn't pick me out especially for such loving attention. He acted the same with Kathy. Maybe even with Carole, who was more resistant—our mother's favorite baby girl and not a Daddy's girl like us. Such intimacy didn't bother Kathy—she welcomed it—but it drove me further into myself. At eleven and a half, after beginning to menstruate and developing breasts, which my father gleefully pointed out to visiting family and friends, I backed away from his embraces and have paid the price ever after, rarely being able to abandon myself absolutely to any man. I resorted to the mantra I'd used as a child to resist my mother's kisses—"Don't touch me!"

"You're always holding something back," Dave once told me. He was right. Unless I'm stoned or loosened up with drink or madly in love or lust, I have trouble giving myself away without stint, sexually or otherwise. It is not my father's fault, since he was true to his character—intense and sexual in every aspect of his being. It was likely the conundrum of an eldest child, wanting to be in control or afraid of being out of control, excited to be at the edge but hesitant to jump.

I said nothing about my suspicions to my mother or father or sisters because I assumed the Korean teenager would protect herself as I had protected myself, but while the incest taboo inhibited me, it did not work for a plain girl hungry for affection and alien in blood, personality, and culture. As for my father, like many macho men in their seventies, he must have been enchanted by the tease of a young and adoring girl. Maybe he was overwhelmed by feelings he thought had fled with age. I'm sure he felt a surge of manhood that could invigorate his life.

The situation was made trickier because the Korean girl's older sisters and their families had become a second family. Mom cooked chicken paprikás for their clan and bragged that their children called her Grandmother. My father invited the Koreans to weekends at our beach house, and back in Chicago the adopted family reciprocated. Years later, long gone from my father's house, the girl graduated from college and law school, became engaged, and disappeared in Asia, where she suffered a nervous breakdown. Her family found out about her high school romance with my father and broke contact not only with him but with my mother. This hurt Mom deeply, for she considered herself a victim too.

In hindsight, I think I should have intervened. I might have stopped a lot of grief—or caused a lot of grief—but I would have done what I felt was right at the time. On the other hand, it was none of my business. I would bristle if my kids felt free to intrude into my intimate life uninvited, and they don't want me sticking my nose into theirs.

After my father died, Mom tried to reestablish contact with that Korean family. Strangely, one of them became her hospital cardiologist when she had a heart attack while my father was passing away in a nursing home. But the rapprochement has been cool. Trust was lost and could not be regained. This is why, seventy-five years after she met my father in Paris, fell in love with him, had children, emigrated to Chicago, worked with him, fought with him, bought a house in the dunes, divorced and remarried him, traveled the world on an extended second honeymoon, had grandchildren and great-grandchildren, cared for and buried him, Helene Beck did not want her ashes mingled with Steve Deutch's.

"Are you sure?" Carole asked when she and Mom came back to the cottage with our father's gravestone. Kathy asked the same question a year or so later. Now it's my turn. As her death approaches, Mom has softened. She is able, at last, to dwell on a half-century of love and intimacy as well as betrayal and loss.

"You can bury *some* of my ashes next to his."

Annick's Ashes. I approve my mother's stance on ultimate disposal and, like her, have fidelity issues with my dead husband, who broke my heart more than once. But even if I didn't, I would choose to be divided in death as I have been in life.

I'd like some of my ashes to be buried in an urn beside the casket of Dave Smith in Missoula's old Catholic cemetery. Dave was my first love, my great love, and the father of my children. When he died suddenly at age forty-one, I bought a double plot so I could have a black stone with my name on it placed next to his. I believe our spirits will rest comfortably together near the graves of good friends Dick Hugo, Jim Welch, and Eric Johnson. And our parcel of burying ground has room for more than one set of ashes, so if any or all of our sons decide to rest with us they will be able to do so.

Of the remainder of my ashes, a good handful should be mingled with Bill Kittredge's, depending on who dies first. Bill has been my lover, companion, and partner for more than thirty years and will likely choose to be scattered over the high desert in Oregon's Warner Valley where he grew up and where his heart remains. I fancy a share of me should go with him to drift among sagebrush on that high plain.

Reserve another handful, please, to be buried on the hillock next to our log house on Bear Creek Road. This is where Rasta and Betty and Bruno rest, where our old cats Ceca and Kevin are buried, and where Lulu, Bruno's younger black Lab companion, will go when her time comes. Place a glaciated rock over me there, surrounded by ground-covering kinnikinnick and strawberries gone wild, and the blue-flowered flax I planted under tall ponderosas.

The rest of my ashes must be tossed into the Big Blackfoot River at Red Rocks. Here, sandy beaches fan from either side of a water-sculpted red rock point. Ponderosas tower over our family's favorite picnic grounds, and the scent of pine mingles with the ozone of water over rock. At Red Rocks, the river pools in jade-green holes, then lightens to aquamarine as it riffles over maroon stones in a rush downstream. What gives the place its name is a tall iron-hued cliff that juts into the current on the opposite shore. That red cliff is embroidered with chartreuse lichen. It anchors small firs in its fissures.

In summers after I became a widow, at a yearly hoopla called the Blackfoot Boogie, I danced with my sons and our friends on a meadow behind the cliff to a rousing mix of country and western and hillbilly rock played by the Mission Mountain Wood Band. We drank beer, smoked pot, and many (not I) plunged naked off the cliff into the river. Today, no public orgies are permitted on those public lands, but Red Rocks is still my paradise: it offers haven for flabby, gray-haired, never-say-die nudists; for college kids with stick-chasing mutts; for fly fishermen in rubber rafts or guide boats; for tots and their moms and giggling teens in inner tubes; and for grandmas like me and my friend Jean packing in deviled eggs and white wine while our dogs and grandkids cavort in cool waters.

Any season will do for the throwing of ashes. What matters is the emptying. Like my mother, I yearn to be scattered in waters. I want to be pulled seaward from the place I call sacred. Whirled in currents bit by bit and bone by bone.

May Flowers. This morning is misty and cool and fragrant with spring in full bloom. Wildflowers are thick in the woods and bright as confetti around the house. As Bruno and I saunter wherever our feet take us, I study the flowers as a way of meditation. And to my dog's confusion, I speak their names out loud.

"Trillium," I say. Bruno turns his head as if I am speaking to him. Trillium shine like large stars in the deep green understory of the forest: three oblong white petals sitting high on a stout stem above three whorled leaves. They are the most flagrant of blossoms whose hearts or mouths or sexual organs turn pink as they mature, ripening toward magenta before the petals wither. Trillium is a lily but reminds me of orchids. When we came to Sawyer for my birthdays in May, they would be blooming on the hillside along our stairway, as they are blooming today. Mom would pick a large bouquet and set them in a vase by my birthday cake. I came to think of trillium as my totem flower.

Wild columbine grows almost a foot high along our terrace wall and down the flagstone path toward the beach where Bruno and I are heading despite a sprinkle of rain. *Columbine* is a word I like to enunciate. It brings Shakespeare to mind and Elizabethan songs, graceful and elegantly flowing. Its red-orange petals are yellow at the heart and tipped with yellow stamens. The blossoms bell from slender stems above lobed leaflets. I have no urge to pick this flower with the lovely name. It is too delicate, wild, and perfectly at home.

In shady nooks alongside the cottage's foundation and scattered under oaks and maples near my father's gravestone I find clumps of lily of the valley. I am not sure these are true wildflowers. Their waxy, bell-like blossoms are lined up along their stems and give off the same fresh, sweet odor as the domestic variety that grew under lilacs in the backyards of our apartment on Lakeside Street and the house in Wilmette. "Lily of the valley" rolls from my tongue like poetry. It is an old-fashioned flower—Victorian—like my grandmothers Beck and Deutch, whose favorite it was. We girls would buy cheap, pungent lily of the valley cologne for their birthdays. The old ladies splashed the scent behind their necks and along their soft, wrinkled arms. The fragrance lingered in their handkerchiefs, blouses, and carefully folded silken lingerie.

Tramping across the grassy clearing that passes as a lawn in front of our cottage's kitchen door, Bruno and I brush by a scatter of weedy plants with pink flowers on hairy stems. "Wild geranium," I exclaim. I am familiar with this species because it grows in Montana's pine forests, but we do not see these wildflowers in our high cold country until late June. I have read that their proper name refers to the beaky shape of the fruit—*geranium* being Greek for crane—but see nothing crane-like about them. When Mom stoops to pulls weeds from this meager patch of grass, she will not pluck the wild geraniums. She will supervise me as I plant purple, pink, and salmon impatiens in the north-facing plot where she always plants them, knowing full well that this is an exercise in impermanence. After we leave there will be no one to tend to the impatiens or water them. The pots of domestic red geraniums we have hung on the porch will also last only a week. We bought them because they remind my mother of Hungary, of Paris. They remind me of her.

Lurking close to the ground in the green shade of a dying hedgerow are small clumps of diminutive purple violets. Their leaves are heart-shaped and their stems are slender, each one rising from the root. Violets are a universal symbol of rebirth, and they grow wild along logging roads above our meadow in Montana. "Violet," I say, thinking this would be a good name for a grandchild or a puppy. Mohammed favored violets, and the Bonaparte emperors chose it to be their emblem. Pale blue to deep purple, these wild ones are too small to make into bouquets like the cultured ones sold on the boulevards of Paris. I pull up my hood, pick a couple, and stick them into the buttonhole of my rain jacket. They will wither and fade before my walk is finished.

Our shower is turning to serious rain, but Bruno and I are not finished with our walk. We duck through tall grasses and chokecherry brush in the fore dunes above the beach, detouring across a sandy clearing below our deceased neighbor's empty house. Here, lilacs grow in high bushes with spreading arms. They are going wild, since no one pays any attention to them. "Lilacs do not in

our dooryard bloom," I say to myself, stealing from Walt Whit-
man. It is too shady for them to thrive on our hilltop, but down
in this sheltered, sunny cove the bushes are thick with lavender
blossoms. I will come back after the rain lets up to steal an armful
for my mother, for she delights in lilacs as much as I do. Their
heady scent will flow from the green vase on the dining-room
table, wafting into the kitchen to duel with odors of Mom's roast
pork, garlic, beans, and applesauce.

Dog Music. It is midnight. Mom and I have watched all the TV
a person can stand—especially me. She has slept on the couch
most of the evening. Jerking awake, she pretends to pay attention
but can't make out what the characters are saying. Even so, I have
to coax her upstairs, since she holds fast to the habit of staying
up as long as her children do. Finally, my mother finishes her
ablutions, takes out her hearing aids and removes her bridges,
brushing each false tooth with immaculate care. Before covering
herself with a thin nightgown, she stands naked by the bathroom
sink—a gnomish, hunched, and breastless crone.

Mom lost her breasts in a double mastectomy when she was
sixty-one. I was in England at the time with Dave, Eric, and
Steve, having just given birth to the twins, and knew nothing
about the surgery. In typical fashion, our parents had not let their
daughters in on the bad news until the crisis was past. "We didn't
want you to be worried," they said.

The decision for radical surgery was pushed on Mom by our
elderly Hungarian surgeon and my father—men deciding to cut
off a woman's breasts. It was an operation my sisters and I might
have fought, since my mother did not have cancer, only a dangerous precancerous condition in the tissues surrounding her nip-
ples. Today, there might be solutions less invasive. But thinking
back, I have to admit the men's decision may have been the safest

route, for here my mother stands almost forty years later, strong and relatively healthy, while both of them are dead.

I kiss Mom's cheek. It is a sunken cavity without the infrastructure of false teeth. Although I usually disdain the beauty masks of makeup and Botox, my mother has taught me to open my mind to realities more complex than authenticity. The exposed flesh and bones of her disintegrating body do not reveal her true self. Her essence resides in her eyes, which are still bright and inquisitive. The rest of what she shows to the world is artifice. Mother loves beauty beyond anything except babies (to her, all babies are beautiful), and if she can no longer aspire to beauty, she can create a persona that implies it—a woman well groomed, well dressed, and well coiffed. That's why she is obsessive about her toilette. Obsessive to the edge of madness.

"Go to bed, Mom." I take the brush from her hands and turn her away from the bathroom mirror. I kiss her much-brushed white hair and lead her past the stairway to her bedroom. She climbs into the double bed with its bird's-eye maple frame designed by my father and signals for me to close her door.

I wash quickly, then lie down in the adjoining room in the single bed I have had since childhood, relishing the new mattress. A thin wooden wall separates me from the head of my mother's bed. Sleeping so close was a problem when she could hear, for Mom was alert to any of us sneaking downstairs for illicit adventures, or me and Kathy (who slept in the twin bed across the room) giggling and whispering or reading till dawn with a flashlight under the covers.

These days she hears nothing, but I do. I put a pillow between my ear and the wall, trying not to listen to her heavy breathing, snores, gasps, and coughs. I know she will grope her way to take a pee in the morning's early hours, and I hope she can hold it until she reaches the toilet, and I pray she does not trip and fall down the stairs. If all goes well, she may return to bed and sleep until noon.

"So, these are the golden years!" Bill's father, Oscar, said to me and to Bill when his rancher's strong body had been reduced to skin and bones in an Oregon nursing home. I remember the shock of opening the door to his room and surprising him naked on his bed, a breathing skeleton. "He's going to die soon," I whispered to Bill. Bill was in denial. When we came back half an hour later, Oscar was dressed and washed and sitting in a wheelchair. He smiled and said, "I'm going home soon."

"Getting old is not for the faint of heart," I tell Bruno. He looks up at me, pleading. "Sure, boy." He jumps to my side, lays his massive head in my lap—a ninety-pound beast with warm, sweet breath (for a dog). We snuggle a couple of moments and then, because he knows this is a forbidden pleasure, Bruno jumps down to his rug on the floor. Above my head, white ruffled curtains sway in a breeze made cool by wafting over water. The strum of waves is like blood pulsing in arteries. I need some calming influence, so I decide to read Bruno his second poem, settling on a lyric that's more on the money for me than for him. Written by Robert Dana, it provides the title for the collection *Dog Music: Poetry about Dogs*, edited by Joseph Duemer and Jim Simmerman. Jim signed the book for me at a conference in Flagstaff, Arizona, after I told him I was writing a memoir featuring my chocolate Lab. It was the first time I'd met him, and I did not know he was suffering from extreme arthritis and would soon have two hip replacements.

A couple of years later, I was desolated to hear his pain had never abated and that this generous poet had committed suicide at the age of fifty-four. "He loved poetry and stray dogs" is what his colleague Allen Woodman wrote in memorial from Northern Arizona University, where Simmerman held a Regent's chair.

Dog Music

ROBERT DANA

Was it worth it, I ask myself—
all those years of making music
for the deaf? All those somber
and brilliant colors worked
onto canvases for the blind?
Maybe I was composing in a key
only dogs could hear, or cats.
Colors for the multifaceted
eyes of spiders, ants, or flies.
Maybe it was art for saints.
So what if fame is ash; summer
smoke. How much do you need?

HOUSE IN THE DUNES

DAYS SIX TO TWELVE, MAY 16–22

Birds on the Wing. These are Sawyer days, heady and restful, filled with sun and wind, good country food, and visitors from far away. Along the beach, gulls and crows dive for plunder. I spot a great blue heron. A turkey vulture circles with wings outspread, tips feathered like open fingers. At the feeder in the yard, sparrows and robins vie for seeds with fat, thieving squirrels. Courting male cardinals flash scarlet among elms, marking territory with song, while raucous blue jays warn danger to every nestling.

I sit in the wicker rocker on the screened-in porch watching a hairy woodpecker drill for bugs. The orange and black of a monarch butterfly catches my eye. I wonder where the orange and black orioles have gone and if they, like the monarchs, are endangered. I fear for their safety. Birds on the wing pass from our sight like the years I lose track of. Bright feathers. Spring rain in the oaks.

Soon my niece Celia will arrive from Brooklyn, where my son Andrew was also living when I began this journey. Celia is Carole's daughter, an artist and an aspiring writer. I would not put her into this story if it were a novel; I would instead write a character based on Andrew, who witnessed the smoke and devastation of 9/11. Andrew chides me for never visiting while he lived in New York, and I regret my neglect. But this is not a novel and Andrew is back home in Montana, so you must be prepared for actual visitors who enter briefly and then disappear, flying in from the blue and out, like passing birds.

Celia arrives at Michigan City on the bus from O'Hare. Bruno greets her with a moan of excitement and a lick on the face. He loves men but saves his special joy for young women. Maybe his girl love began with the exuberance of my granddaughter Jessy's kisses when he was newborn. Maybe it is the smell of girls, the timbre of their voices. Who knows the heart of a dog?

When we get to the cottage, Bruno muscles Mom out of the way. He rolls on his back, feet up in tummy-rub position. He grins his dog grin. "He's not a dog," Ceal laughs. "He's a big cat!" Celia is a cat person and catlike in her ways, with heavy eyebrows, luminous gray eyes, and a prominent dimpled chin.

"She is my soul mate," says Mom, referring to this grand-daughter's orneriness, intelligence, humor, and style. I, too, have a special kinship with Celia. Like me, she is an artist, a bookworm, well versed in irony, and a sometimes rebel from the middle class (although neither of us rebels against fine food, a home full of grace, or nice shoes). But where I am relatively laid back (for a Deutch), Celia is highly strung. At thirteen, she was a promising student at the San Francisco Ballet's elite school. She decided not to dedicate her life to dance and shaved off her waist-length black hair, dyed the stubble green and pink, and became a punk who hung out on Market Street.

"She's in love," says Mom, glowing more than Celia, who is glowing plenty. Mom's greatest wish is to marry off her unwed grandchildren and incite them to produce a batch of great-grand-children to add to the four she already has. When I learned about Celia's Cuban lover, Jorge, I could not have guessed that within a few years she would be married to him and they would produce a son and a daughter, then struggle through a tough divorce.

"Go to the beach." Mom issues her ritual order, and Celia and I are happy to obey. We throw sticks into the lake for Bruno, and he retrieves them while we catch up on family gossip. Several yards ahead of us he stops in mid-motion, legs splayed, eyes alert, then explodes down the strand toward a faraway dog and his master. I run after him calling and whistling, and so does Celia, but Bruno ignores us. He loves to charge after other dogs like a freight train, then puts on the brakes when he closes in, his thick tail wagging.

The man with the dog backs away, clearly frightened. He holds his spaniel close on a leash. "I'm sorry," I say, grabbing at Bruno's collar, "he's just too friendly."

"If you can't control him, you might keep him on a leash," says the man, turning away in anger.

He is right, but I haven't brought a leash. I pull Brunie's ears, and tell him he's a "bad dog." He hangs his head in false servility. It doesn't last. When I let go of his collar my bad boy runs away into the dunes following a scent. I call and whistle, but although he stays in sight, he does not come. I'm annoyed but not worried because I know Bruno will return. He returns to me because he wants to. He returns out of love or duty, heeding a sense of responsibility that all hunting dogs must have, knowing his job is to range and fetch and come back to his human.

With his soft mouth and mellow temper, Bruno would be a swell hunter if trained by someone who possesses the authority to say "No" or "Yes" or "Come" or "Stay" in a direct way that makes creatures obey. That would not be me. I am a master of mixed messages, and discipline is one of my weaknesses. For most of my life I was not able to discipline myself to punctuality or obedience, much less my children, or students, or dogs. Perhaps that's because I was devoting too much energy to the complex, contradictory, often duplicitous arts of pleasing others—parents, children, husbands, dogs, teachers, and strangers—while at the same time being defensive about preserving my independence and sense of selfhood.

Nine years have passed since Bruno was four and frisky on that beach. He is dead and I am older, with little compunction to please anyone except my grandchildren. A certain authority has also arrived uncalled for, and a measure of discipline with it. I am usually on time these days; my granddaughters sort of abide by my rules; and Lulu tends to come when she is called. Of course you will notice all those qualifiers. And of course I can't take full credit, since the girls are trying to please me, and Lulu—like her mistress—is getting tired of rebellion.

The News about Pat. After dinner, Bill calls. Usually he rings me up around 8:30 a.m., taking a break from his writing. Afternoons, he plays golf. Evenings he cooks a rib steak on his George Foreman grill and drinks several glasses of white wine, or goes out for gin and tonics and appetizers with regulars at the Depot Bar and Grill. Bill usually beds down around nine, but it is past ten o'clock and his voice is strained.

"Pat's in the hospital," says Bill. Pat is his younger brother, who had recently come to Missoula to live out his senior years in proximity to Bill. "It's his heart. He came to see me this afternoon. And he looked really bad. His face was white. The pain was so tough he could not go on."

Oh boy, I think, it must be serious. An old cowman like Pat does not whine about little pains. Bill says he sent Pat off to the emergency room at St. Patrick's Hospital. Within moments, the doctors raced Pat up to the heart unit and then to the operating room where a surgeon opened his blocked coronary arteries with a couple of stents.

Bill coughs his cigarette cough. "They said he was about to have a major heart attack." A pause and what might be a chuckle. "Guess he dodged that bullet."

Just my age, Pat Kittredge is tall and broad shouldered, athletic and shambling at the same time. He is heavy-bellied like

Bill, but his legs are longer and his head is smaller with thinning white hair. Lately, having lost his front two teeth and despising the removable bridge he's supposed to wear, Pat's gap-toothed smile makes him look ingenuous as a boy.

I liked Pat from the first time I met him at the Eastgate Lounge and Liquor Store more than thirty years ago. The Eastgate was a watering hole where Missoula's mostly macho literati gathered in the seventies. Bill held court there surrounded by his graduate students. Located across from a shopping center and the nearest bar to the university, the Eastgate was a workingman's place with velvet girlie wall art, a foosball table, pinball machines, a Formica-topped bar, spunky women bartenders, a jukebox filled with country and western music, and an adjoining liquor store.

Pat had escaped a bad marriage and moved from Oregon to Missoula with his young son, Chris. He wanted in on the partying and the camaraderie. I did, too, for though I loved the solitude of my house on Bear Creek, after Dave died, the isolation could bring me down. So I'd go to the Eastgate where the fun seemed nonstop. Bill was usually there, but he frightened me with his unpredictable, inebriated energy. Pat seemed more normal. I liked his ironic self-effacement, cowboy manners, and the intelligence in his blue eyes. He was wary of women, "snakebit," as Bill would say, but Pat and I had an easy rapport. Mutual friends wanted to set me up with him, but the chemistry was wrong. Now, we are comfy being just good old friends.

"Oh my God! How's he doing?"

"Better. But his heart isn't working like it should. I guess some damage was done."

Bill can't keep the worry out of his voice. It was Bill who insisted that Pat move to Missoula from Boise, where he'd been living in self-imposed exile as the janitor for a public school. And it was Bill who paid the moving expenses. Pat did not resist. He and Bill are each other's best friends and closest family, and both are obsessed with golf. They play together and talk afterward about things they would not discuss with anyone else, laughing at jokes funny only to each other. It's the kind of boy intimacy shared by my identical twins.

We'd known all spring that something was wrong with Pat. He'd been complaining for weeks about a pain in his back that no chiropractors or anti-inflammatory drugs could relieve. His exhaustion showed in the hollows under his eyes, a chalky pallor, and the stoop in his gait. Pat has worked many jobs, including a stint as a lawyer, and his most recent is mopping and polishing floors at the university. Bill and I attributed his aches to a much-used body rebelling at work too hard for a man in his mid-sixties. The doctor Pat went to see examined him cursorily and said, "Take Advil."

The last time I saw Pat we played golf at the Missoula Country Club on a bluebird afternoon in early spring. Bill always rides in a golf cart and Pat walks, but this day he decided to ride. When we reached the fourth tee, Pat ran to the bathroom in a caretaker's shed. He was gone a long time and came back pale and shaken.

"Do you think it could be his heart?" I whispered to Bill. When my mother had a heart attack while my father was on his deathbed, her symptoms were back pain, shortness of breath, and extreme tiredness. Bill shrugged. Now Pat is in the hospital and Bill is distraught. Two thousand miles away, I can do nothing.

In the Meantime. It is May 18, my son Steve's forty-sixth birthday. Steve is dog- and house-sitting at the ranch, and Mom, Celia, and I call him, singing "Happy Birthday" off-key. I wince at the idea that he is approaching middle age. With his smooth-shaven face and cropped brown hair, Steve seems younger than his years. A converted and conservative Catholic, he is my most overtly spiritual son.

"I went to see Pat in the hospital," says Steve. Pat and Steve are unlikely friends. Opposites in faith, background, and personality, they are nevertheless alike in their unworldliness and alike in their aloneness. I imagine them in Pat's sterile hospital room like characters in a Beckett drama—two big hearted guys stranded in a bachelorhood of the soul. "Pat's heartbeat is still irregular," says Steve. "And the doctors are making him stay until it starts working right."

I wonder if being younger brothers of dominant siblings connects Pat and Steve. Or if the common factor is psychic struggle and lost years. But where Steve is eager to carve a middle-class life for himself as a government man in the Bureau of Land Management (BLM), Pat has divested himself of ambition and worldly possessions. Twenty years or so ago, he went to law school. Like Steve, he was in his forties and attempting to start over. He decided to practice law in Klamath Falls, Oregon, where he and Bill had gone to high school.

"That was a goddamn mistake," said their father, Oscar. Bill agreed. In Klamath, Pat fell in with his hard-drinking high school buddies. He struggled to maintain a criminal law practice, suffered from diabetes and depression, and got in trouble with his sister, Roberta, for appropriating funds from his father's estate as its executor. She sued him and he was disbarred. They haven't spoken to each other since.

"I was never happy being a lawyer," Pat told Steve from his hospital bed. "There is no peace to be found there."

Leaving Us to Weep. My mother's French friend, Marie Jeanne, arrives. Marie Jeanne is a widow a bit older than I am with short hair dyed black and heavy eyebrows. Mom loves talking French with Marie Jeanne, as she does with Victoria. The language turns a key in her brain and she revs up into the sharp person we used to know, no longer a confused old gnome asleep on the couch, mouth open and snoring.

On May 20, we have dinner at Café Gulistan, a Turkish restaurant a few miles down the Red Arrow Highway. Marie Jeanne brings a bottle of French champagne and we drink to health and longevity. We cannot know that the Kurdish owner of the restaurant will soon be arrested as a suspected terrorist, or that the Chamber of Commerce and the white, rural community will rally around him, or that he will be held in a Michigan jail until the ACLU comes to his defense.

The Turkish woman serving dinner, the dark-haired little daughter, the smiling proprietor in suit and tie—here we have the American dream. Immigrants escaped from torture and terrors are prospering deep in the countryside of the free world. At the same time, these good people will soon inhabit the American nightmare. But all is not yet lost. When I drive the Red Arrow Highway again in the fall, there will be signs proclaiming *Free Ibrahim* posted in front of businesses and stuck like election placards in the tree-shaded yards of farmers and factory workers.

When we get home the phone is ringing. It's Bill. His voice is choked. "Pat's dead," he says. "Poor Patty . . ." Bill cannot go on.

After many gasping, tear-drowned stops, he tells me the story. Yesterday, Pat had been discharged from the hospital. One part of his heart was still not working right, but the doctor thought he was well enough to go home. He attached a device to Pat's chest that would chart his heartbeats and record them, so at his next visit the doctor would know if the irregularities were continuing.

"It was a great day," said Bill. "Warm and sunny, and Pat wanted to go to the country club with me."

They spent the afternoon together, Bill playing eighteen, Pat kibitzing from the cart. "Couldn't be better," said Bill. But as twilight fell, Pat got chilly and tired. Bill took him home. Next morning Bill telephoned to say hello. Maybe take Pat out for breakfast. There was no answer. He figured Pat had gone out early, as he liked to do. Bill called again later. Still no answer.

And then again. Now he was truly worried. So Bill went over to Pat's apartment. The old Honda was parked out front. The apartment's door was locked. He pounded on the door and called Pat's name. There was no answer. Bill searched until he located the building's supervisor and convinced him to unlock the door.

"He was in bed," said Bill. "He was dead!"

The gizmo on Pat's chest indicated his heart had stopped at 1:30 a.m. He had died, as we say, in his sleep. But what does that mean? Can a person die and be asleep at the same time? I believe there must be an instant of awakening. A breath heaved. A flash of recognition. I wonder if Pat was dreaming when his breath stopped. I wonder if death is a dream interrupted.

My heart squeezes. This is how my husband Dave had died in May 1974, almost exactly thirty years before. "Electrical failure," said the ambulance man. But Dave had not been sleeping. His last words were "Oh, dear." Then he fell. He was dead before he hit the floor. Our six-year-old twins watched from the stairway while I tried to revive their father. They are still trying to recover from the dread of that moment, as am I. And although we cannot know what Dave knew as his heart stopped, I'm sure he felt the knockdown jolt. In his last seconds, Dave experienced the coming of nothing.

All these thoughts jam into my head while Bill is telling his story. What can I say? "Oh, Baby . . . Oh my God . . . I'm so sorry . . . Poor Billy . . . Poor Pat." Language is not sufficient. Sometimes there can be no comfort.

My mother hovers around me, sensing something is badly wrong. I motion her away. She is stubborn in keeping death at bay. Why is she alive at ninety-seven while Pat is dead at sixty-seven, or Dave at forty-one? At least they died quickly, leaving before their time, but leaving painlessly. Leaving us to weep. I am reminded of one of Bill's favorite lines from the Lattimore translation of *The Iliad*. The women are mourning along with

Achilles, "grieving openly for Patroklos." They wail and tear their hair, weeping not so much for the dead, says the poet, but "for her own sorrows each."

Tonight I weep with and for my Billy and for Pat and for myself. The knowledge of loss lies like a raw potato in my craw, but I do not shed many tears. I am a slow person, chronically late, and grief can take days to overwhelm me. A sight or sound will set me off: sun ravishing the branches of red-leafed maples, two waddling old women bundled in furs, a ferruginous hawk screeching from a snow-decked pine, dogtooth violets along the logging road, a Bach cantata, bluebirds. Something clicks in my brain and I want to share it with Dave or my father and, soon, my mother. Then tears fall unstoppable. Such violent surges of grief come in a flash, then go away. But memories remain. As my friend, the Buddhist poet Jane Hirshfield has written:

> Living memory holds the dead as a hand holds water,
> As a dry window keeps the traces of rain.
> And still we speak.

Impressionistic. Celia leaves. Marie Jeanne distracts Mom with their ongoing *Scrabble* competition.

"I have an *S*," says Mom. "I put it here. *Simp!*"

"*Simp* is not a word."

"Yes. I have heard my grandchildren say it!"

Marie Jeanne opens the dictionary. There is no *simp*. Mom will not relent. It's a hilarious duo—the nearly deaf, Hungarian-French-English-speaking centenarian trying to cheat her honest but competitive French friend.

Later we walk down the road to the church-camp picnic area by the stream. Mom and I hold hands and stop often. Tall beeches are in leaf, berry brush blooms, and wildflowers sprinkle yellow and white, blue and pink in the clearing. Bruno is tuned in to our elegiac mood. When we reach the clearing at the end of our road and rest on a picnic bench, he sits at Mother's feet. Marie Jeanne, who is shy of this big animal, pats his head. He puts his heavy paw on her knee. "Good boy," she says.

When we turn to retrace our steps I stand apart, studying the scene. I see us as figures in an impressionist painting. Here is the fractured light. A medley of pastels. The bent old woman leans on her cane. Her companion holds her arm. The daughter walks behind, a brown dog at her heel.

At the cottage I think of Pat all day long. Pat loved to come to the ranch for dinner, to sit on our deck in the warm seasons smoking and drinking gin and tonics with Bill. I have snapshots of Pat leaning back in a red metal chair. He resembles his father, Oscar, who also preferred that chair. We would dip chips into salsa and look out at grazing cattle or down the canyon where Bear Creek runs through timbered slopes toward the Blackfoot River. It must have reminded those men of the MC Ranch in eastern Oregon that each had left behind. But only a little.

"You call this jack pine flat a ranch? There's nothing worth calling a ranch in all of western Montana!" says Bill with the pride of a dispossessed prince.

The ranch the brothers grew up on ran to thousands of acres of plowed meadows planted with grains. Its irrigated marsh-lands harbored white pelicans in head-high grass, and the miles of high, arid sagebrush prairies they leased from the BLM were rimmed by buttes where antelope multiplied in herds of prehistoric dimensions. As boys and young men, Bill and Pat harvested grain by the boxcar load, drank beer with the hired hands, and drove cattle across the desert like the horseback cowboys they were. That western youth stamped Pat indelibly, as it stamped Bill. But Bill could bring the ranch back in stories and essays. Pat had no such release. He couldn't go home to his lost ranch and family, and he couldn't settle down.

The pattern began when Pat flunked out of Stanford, where his father had insisted he go. He felt out of place and refused to attend classes. Then he joined the army, worked on his family's ranch, sold auto parts in Phoenix, owned a western wear store, was twice married and divorced, got a degree in philosophy, went to law school, practiced law, was disbarred, became a grandfather, and ended his life as a janitor.

Pat was my kind of country and western antihero—fair-haired, charming, damaged, self-defeating, smart-assed, and just plain smart. He was a natural athlete and a picture of grace. Pat had been a star baseball player in high school until he wrecked his knee. He was a daunting pool player and a low-handicap golfer. I close my eyes and see him standing tall on an elevated tee. His swing is fluid and elegant. I hear the clean ring of metal striking ball. I see the long arc of his shot flying high and into the blue.

I can't mourn Pat without thinking of Bill. I imagine him sitting on his leather couch in his book-piled apartment in Missoula. The dusty venetian blinds are drawn. His ashtray brims with cigarette butts. His bed is unmade. Framed photos of childhood sprinkle the walls: Bill and Pat in boots and chaps quick-drawing toy pistols; Bill, Pat, and little sister Roberta dangling their feet off the back of a horse-pulled wagon; a portrait of his beloved German blacksmith grandfather in suit and tie; and in the place of honor, his mother, Josephine, peering out of an oval frame, demure in her fur-trimmed coat, her dark hair glowing—nothing like the regal, overweight matron I knew, wearing diamonds and mink, her bleached hair piled in a lacquered beehive.

Bill must be feeling beyond bereft. His father went first. Then his mother. Now Pat. His sister, Roberta, is eight years younger and inhabits a rural, blue-collar Oregon that Bill left behind, and she and Pat were so angry at each other they had not spoken for years. Bill's son Brad and daughter Karen and his four grandsons will surely call offering sympathy. But they are busy with work, school, and family in Portland and Seattle, and if they offer to fly to Missoula, Bill will tell them thanks, but no thanks. Aside from me, he has no one with whom to share his grief. He needs me. And he needs me soon.

Country and Western. May 21. I am driving back roads in southern Michigan from Three Oaks to Sawyer to Bridgman to Stevensville, ostensibly doing errands but mostly just driving. The day is cool and misty, a few showers falling. In this dreamy landscape of undulating hayfields and oak-lined lanes, rain mutes the orchards of apples and peaches while foot-high rows of new corn glisten lime-green as I pass.

Bruno snores in the back of the 4Runner. A Hank Williams CD keeps me company. I have been drawn to Hank's voice since I was a Chicago kid enchanted by westerns. His nasal whiskey drawl played over and over on my radio's country and western station tuned me in to a honky-tonk reality I never could tune out. I sang along with Hank's songs, dreaming of horses and cowboys and busted romances.

I've come a long way down Hank's bluesy road since those teenage days and could write my own songs of heartbreak, but his are best, so I sing with him again on this sad afternoon—wind blowing our words out the open window: "Darling, let's turn back the years." Then the prophetic and ironic "I'll never get out of this world alive." And finally, my favorite, "Your Cheatin' Heart."

The lyrics bring Dave Smith back to me, not Pat or Bill. Dave, who first heard that song when I played the vinyl record for him in our Wilmette house in 1953. He recognized in Hank's plaintive tunes his own emotional landscape and became a fan for life. I was seventeen. Dave was twenty. We were in love.

Much later, in 1967 Montana, Dave and I recorded "Your Cheatin' Heart" in the documentary we were making about Dick Hugo. We were shooting in black-and-white 16mm film with a hand-wound Bolex and no sync sound, filming Hugo's Milltown Bar poem in the actual Milltown Bar. Hank Williams was playing on the jukebox. Sun streamed through an open door. A millworker in a cowboy hat shot pool with the stout poet. For me the song was no longer a bad dream but reality. I was pregnant with the twins. Dave was having a serious extramarital affair with one of our best friends, and his cheatin' heart tore mine in ways that never heal. You can see me in the background. I'm the young woman with cropped black hair whose yellow sundress hides the growing lump of her belly.

Still later, in the early nineties, Bill Kittredge and I made a pilgrimage to the Hank Williams museum in Georgiana, Alabama. The museum is a modest Victorian boarding house where Hank had lived with his mother before going off to Birmingham and Nashville, to fame and disastrous love. In the bedroom was a set of curtains made for him and unfaithful Audrey by a fan. The words were embroidered in black on a yellow field: "When tears come down like fallin' rain . . ."

Fallin' rain splatters my windshield. Tears come down hard. It is Pat I'm crying for now, not Dave anymore. Pat lost his life just when it was turning toward good times. He could have enjoyed many seasons of camaraderie with his brother and friends, living his version of simplicity, a kind of Zen practice. I pull off the road and bow my head to the steering wheel. Bruno, alarmed, jumps into the backseat and nuzzles my neck. The rain eases. I wipe my eyes on my sleeve. I put my foot on the gas. Where are you now, Patty-boy?

Turkey Feathers. May 22. I repair the hole in the porch screen. I buy Listerine for Mom. Finally, I go to Drier's butcher shop in Three Oaks, which has become a monument to sausage. Its plank floors are sprinkled with sawdust, and the worn counter displays a historic preservation plaque. In photos from the century before, stout men in blood-spattered aprons sport handlebar mustaches. A horse-drawn meat wagon waits on the cobbled street. Women in feather-trimmed hats are bargaining at this counter. Today the women wear jeans, and with fame, prices have risen, but the liverwurst and baloney, bratwurst and homemade mustards are tasty as ever. I buy some of each to put on ice and bring back as presents for Bill and Steve.

Three Oaks is spruced up these days. The old Featherbone Factory in the center of town, where turkey feathers were processed into struts for girdles after whalebone became rare, is a mall with boutiques, curios, and a drama society that puts on plays. On Main Street I notice that the restored Vickers Theatre is now also on the National Register of Historic Places. When we were kids, Kathy and Carole and I would go to the Vickers with our parents on a Saturday night to see the latest Hollywood film noir with Humphrey Bogart or Alan Ladd. Carole was too little to care about such things, but Kathy and I would dress in short shorts and our sexiest T-shirts, sneak a little lipstick, and sit in the back row away from our parents so we could trade goo-goo eyes with the local boys. The Vickers of old was dimly lit and had sticky floors. Now the lobby glows with refinished oak and glass, and the films are arty and foreign. Being part of recorded history makes me feel old, too, but I'm ready for escape, and even if she misses most of the dialogue, I think Mom might enjoy *Being Victor Vargas*. I decide to take her to the seven o'clock show.

Bad idea. Mom does not comprehend the dialogue, and she misinterprets what she sees. "That girl was seducing the boy," she says. "I don't like her."

"She was the girl he wanted. She is being kind to him. He wants her to be his girlfriend."

"I hate women!"

"Why?" I suppress a smile. "Why do you hate women?"

"They are always seducing the men."

I'm not willing to step into this booby trap. "What do you want to eat?"

The Italian restaurant where we wait for a late dinner is bustling with moviegoers. I order a glass of red wine and one for Mom. She studies the menu for ten minutes. When our order finally arrives, the salads are ordinary and the pasta bland. Mom takes an hour to eat, cutting every shard of her meatballs, taking the seeds out of the cucumbers. I drink my wine, order another, then finish most of hers. By the time we leave, both of us are tired and cranky, not because of the movie or food, but because our time together in the safe nest of Sawyer has been cut short.

Loading Up. May 23 is a sunny morning and Mom is asleep. I take Bruno to the beach. He is excited, not knowing this will be his final dip. We turn toward the state park where dogs are forbidden, but what the hell. It's my last beach walk, too.

Four miles north, the domes of Bridgman's nuclear plant glint silver in the sun, ominous in their beauty. The beach is deserted, as are the trails through the dunes and the three concession stands that loom like octagonal concrete mushrooms at the base of Mount Baldy. Crows call from silvered cottonwood snags at Baldy's crown.

When we were children, Baldy was our Mount Everest. With my sisters and the Burns kids I would climb to the top, ravenous for the peanut butter and jam sandwiches, fresh peaches, and warm jars of lemonade that hung heavy in my rucksack. Hopping around patches of poison ivy, our little gang explored back trails through pines and played cowboys and Indians in the dappled shade of those now-dead cottonwoods. Then we'd run, tumble, roll, and somersault down the sandy slopes, race across the hot asphalt of the parking lot, and leap into the lake.

This morning Brunie stays close. He halfheartedly charges a cluster of sandpipers. They spray at our approach, gather and wheel, catch the sun in a dazzle of wings. A ranger on a four-wheeler comes after us.

"No dogs on the beach," he says.

"Oh, I didn't know," I lie.

I'd like to wait for the sun to warm me enough for a swim. A few years ago, I would have stripped naked and dived in no matter how cold the weather or water. Now, I feel no need to freeze my old ass. Opting for comfort marks a new stage of aging. Wonder why I waited so long?

When I get back to the cottage, Mom is miraculously up and finished with her toilette. We eat the last bit of coffee cake from the Swedish bakery, sip at our coffees, and pack up leftovers to take back to Chicago.

We get to the Breakers around noon and Mom gives Bruno a goodbye hug. He will stay locked in the car while I drop her and her bags off at the apartment, but in typical Jewish mom fashion, she won't allow me to leave until I eat. The sandwich she laboriously puts together is the ultimate Helene Deutch concoction. The bread is Jewish rye with caraway seeds. It is slathered with *kurozott* and topped with Drier's baloney and hard salami. Sliced green pepper and rounds of cucumber are finishing touches. This is the sandwich Mom packed into lunchboxes when I was a girl. The other kids with their peanut butter and jelly on white bread turned up their noses, disgusted by the odors issuing from my lunch. Sometimes I never opened it and went hungry, ashamed of being foreign and different.

In later years, Mom would wrap the same combination in plastic and stuff the sandwiches into a paper bag, adding an apple and some homemade cookies for us to take on airplanes or trains or car trips. And still today, on hot afternoons in Sawyer, my sisters, kids, and grandkids, damp from swimming in the lake, will be served make-your-own versions on the screened-in porch. We call it our "Sawyer lunch."

The moment to kiss my mother goodbye inevitably arrives. As I bend to her face, the odor I inhale is not an old person's sour scent but the clean, fresh smell I associate only with Mom: face powder and French cologne, a hint of Pond's cold cream, and Listerine.

She reaches up to hug me. Her arms are long for her hunched, short-waisted body with its hummock of stomach. Her red-rimmed eyes are moist. I feel weepy myself.

"Thank you, Annickam."

"Thank you, Momushka."

"It was too short," she says. I nod. It is always too short.

Each of us knows this goodbye could be our last. My heart tells me our time together should not be over, but my nerves have reached their care-giving limits. Truth be told, it is a relief to be walking out the door. Caring for others is a job I have never been able to do well full time. And keeping a smiley face while answering to the demands of this sometimes enchanting, sometimes infuriating, but always needy mother has taken its toll. We walk to the elevator holding hands. "See you in three months," I say.

If all goes well, I'll fly back in the fall. In the meantime Kathy will come this summer, and Carole will follow. Both will bring their daughters and grandkids, and Mom will get to spend precious days at the beach, days with her great-grandchildren. For me, it's back to the road and the ranch, free for a while from the burdens of dealing with extreme old age, oncoming death, and death its own self.

As the elevator whisks me down thirty-two floors, I imagine how satisfying it will be to leave the oppressive air of the Breakers and hit highways going west. Ah, the open road! Me and Bruno running silent across the endless *now* of the plains.

RETURN

DAYS THIRTEEN AND
FOURTEEN, MAY 23–24

The Way Out. In the 4Runner, I study a map of Chicago and discover a way out of town that does not involve a maze of freeways. I take Irving Park, which is Highway 19 and runs clear to Elgin. Big mistake. Drab two- and three-story brick or frame buildings stretch on both sides for miles. Towns called Norridge, Schiller Park, Wood Dale, and Medinah slip by. This humdrum sprawl is the doughy center of the city, home to every era's immigrants and the working poor. Here there are no fanciful skyscrapers. No yacht basins, tree-lined beaches, five-star hotels, galleries, symphonies, museums, and posh restaurants. I wonder what the inhabitants feel about the discrepancy. Maybe they want out, as I do.

Bruno lies in his bed in the back of the SUV. I race through yellow lights, brake abruptly, then jerk ahead. He complains with a moan or a whimper. We approach Elgin, forty miles west of Chicago. Elgin's white man's history goes back to the Black Hawk War of 1833. That's when General Winfield Scott emptied the Fox River Valley of its Pottawattamie inhabitants. Soon after, Yankee veterans returned with their families to settle on the Illinois frontier's rich soil. Borden's condensed milk was manufactured in Elgin, and so were the world-famous watches assembled in the factory that supported the town. Elgin Baylor, the basketball great, got his name, I'm told, because his father, sitting in a hospital waiting room while his wife was in labor, kept checking his Elgin watch. When the nurse announced, "It's a boy," Mr. Baylor said, "We'll name him Elgin."

The city has pre-Victorian cobblestone houses, Queen Anne–style mansions, and Sears & Roebuck prefab houses from the twenties, but what interests me is the Northern Illinois Hospital and Asylum for the Insane. Built in 1872, the mental hospital's slate-roofed buildings were torn down recently, but they are vivid in my mind. When I was twelve my father took me to the Elgin asylum to visit his (and therefore my) cousin Paul. My little sisters may have been with us (they remember visiting the hospital), but they do not figure in this memory.

"Paul has a sickness called schizophrenia," my father explained. "It makes him confused. Sometimes he hears voices that are not there. Sometimes he has hallucinations. You know, like dreams, except he is awake."

My father would have been shocked to know that in his final years, he too would suffer from hallucinations caused by dementia. "There are little people under my chair," he'd tell me when I came to Chicago to help care for him. He pointed to the wooden base of his La-Z-Boy recliner. "The men are wearing checkered pants and porkpie hats. They are going to kidnap your mother."

A few days later, he insisted that my mother take him in his wheelchair down to their apartment house's manager. "Your daddy was angry," she says. "He wanted a policeman to come upstairs and arrest them. Those little peoples. He could not sleep. He would not let me sleep."

Little people were not Paul's problem. The last of the Deutch family to emigrate from Hungary, he had followed his sister Julia to Chicago, where my father and his surviving older brother, Gene, were already established. Gene and Julia had been in love since childhood but forbidden to marry since they were first cousins. Julia divorced her first husband after settling in the United

States. Freed from traditional restraints, she eloped with Gene to South Carolina, where it was legal for first cousins to marry. Soon they'd have three daughters and would live near us in Chicago and then Wilmette, but I don't know how close they were to their cousin/brother Paul. Especially after he got in trouble.

Paul became an American citizen through an arranged marriage/divorce to a distant niece of my grandmother Deutch, and settled in Chicago with the rest of the Deutch clan. When we went to war with Germany, he joined a U.S. infantry regiment. My father had tried to enlist but was refused because he was too old. He was told he'd be more valuable as a photographer on the home front, so he made recruiting posters for Uncle Sam and became the air-raid warden of Lakeside Street, patrolling our block during blackouts, sporting a helmet, an armband, and a flashlight.

Paul had a real uniform. I remember him as a young, slim, dark, and dashing soldier who came to visit us from boot camp, and again before he was shipped overseas. I was seven and he was the only soldier I knew. I rode him like a horse in our living room and tried on his army hat and believed I was his favorite girl. Maybe I was, because after being wounded in action, Paul gave me his purple heart. Then we lost track of him. It seems he went AWOL, changed his name to Paul Armstrong (after "Jack Armstrong, the All-American Boy" of radio fame), and disappeared into schizophrenia and homeless wandering, working as a dishwasher in greasy spoons all over the South until he cracked up and was sent to the insane ward of a veterans' hospital in Kentucky. There, he fell into catatonia until the discovery of antipsychotic drugs such as Haldol brought him back to a semi-functional state.

My father tracked Paul down and convinced the VA to transfer him to the hospital in Elgin, which was near to his relatives and former home. I remember high gates guarding the asylum and the park-like grounds. Victorian red-brick buildings loomed in winter dusk, mirroring madhouses I'd seen in horror movies. I walked tentatively behind my father, scared to encounter an insane relative I once had loved.

We entered a brightly lit parlor outfitted with sofas, armchairs, and gaming tables. My father and I headed for a round table where a heavy-set man with a five o'clock shadow sat twisting his hands. This slow-speaking, overweight person was not the "uncle" I had loved. That Paul had deep-brown, inquisitive eyes and an aquiline nose like my father's. This Paul had a bulbous nose. His hair was sparse and receding, and the baggy eyes that studied me were drugged and dim. And yet he smiled to see us, so happy we had taken the trouble to visit.

Paul kissed me on the lips, me doing my best not to recoil. My overactive imagination, stimulated by books and movies, had led me to expect some mind-opening revelation from a man of my blood deemed insane. I did not expect small talk. Paul spoke with a heavy Hungarian accent.

"And how do you like your school?" His words were halting due to the zombie effect of his medication.

"Fine, I guess." I could not ask the question I needed to ask. *What is it like to be insane?*

We visited Paul at the asylum a couple of times more before he was released to a halfway house in Chicago. After that, on special occasions, my father would pick him up and bring him to dinner at our house in Wilmette. Usually Aunt Julia and her daughters would join us, but she seemed uncomfortable with her transformed brother. Perhaps ashamed. Although I know she loved him deeply.

I was a freshman at Cornell University when Paul got in trouble at his halfway house for peeping into windows at women, and later that year he was busted for flashing. This news did not horrify me. It just made me sad. Paul was lonesome and horny, and though it is politically incorrect, I believed and still believe that his benign perversity hurt no one. He was not sent back to Elgin but was closely watched and probably dosed with saltpeter. The last time Kathy saw him (I never saw him after I went to Cornell) was before she went off to the University of Michigan. She and my father had come to visit Paul. They brought a gift of Hungarian cookies my mother had baked.

"He grabbed that bag and gobbled them up," Kat told me. "Every one. Tried to talk with his mouth full. It was disgusting. There was slobber all over his chin, crumbs on his belly. I couldn't watch."

A couple of years after Kathy's visit, Paul choked on a finger-long hunk of steak and died instantly. It was hunger that got him. Hunger for women. Red meat. Sweets. Hunger for all the lost years—the life he could never regain.

Driftless Zone. We veer onto Highway 20 in Elgin, but the going is slow until we bypass Rockford. Bruno would like to get out, but I know he can hold it. The bladder control of healthy dogs is impressive to an older woman whose functions demand relief right now! Such retention is not as necessary for my survival as it is for den animals. Dogs in the wild could not allow tell-tale scents to lead predators to their dens. Even puppies will not foul their sleeping quarters. You'd think such instincts would be necessary for humans too, given our origins in caves and compounds, but we seem to have lost those genes on the way to flush toilets.

The most radical incident of dog self-control I know of happened with our German shepherd Sylvie when we lived in Seattle in the sixties. Dave and I had decided to take Eric and Steve on a two-day hike along the wild beaches of Olympic National Park. We piled out of our green Volkswagen bus into the Lake Ozette parking lot, hefted our backpacks, hooked Sylvie to her leash, and headed down the trail. That's when we saw the No Dogs Allowed sign. As luck would have it, a park ranger was coming toward us up the trail, so we turned back.

The boys were near to tears, and Dave and I were disappointed, so we locked Sylvie into the bus and settled her on a mat of newspapers with a pail full of water and a pile of food. If she dirtied the car, we'd clean it up. During the next two days while climbing headlands, exploring tide pools, and maneuvering across huge, slippery driftwood logs, I worried about our dog. But when we'd hiked the boggy three-mile trail back to the parking lot and opened the bus's back door, Sylvie jumped out, wagged her tail, licked the boys, and trotted into the forest. Her water bowl was empty, her food gone, but there was not a drop of urine or speck of excrement anywhere in the vehicle.

Bruno and I approach the Mississippi Valley. We have driven into the far corner of Illinois where it borders Wisconsin to the north and Iowa to the east, and I find no rest stops, no sheltering trees. Flatlands begin to rock and roll, and we enter a landscape known as the Driftless Zone. The name sounds like a rock band but denotes a singular region in the Midwest that was left free of glaciers during recent ice ages. As a result, this countryside does not have the deep rich loess soil that makes agriculture thrive on the Illinois prairies. What it has is exposed rock and a lead mining industry that began with local Indians, continued with the French as early as 1690, and made the nearby town of Galena rich and more populous than Chicago in the mid-1800s.

I spot Charles Mound to the north, at 1,235 feet, the highest point in the state. Southward the land breaks off into palisades that fall into the Mississippi's chasm. Above those palisades is Chestnut Mountain, which boasts a ski area. I am amused at the notion of a ski area rising from this pancake Midwest, but the Chestnut Hill complex has a 475-foot vertical drop to the braided, island-studded channels of the Great River, and a seven-acre terrain park for snowboarders, jumpers, and acrobatic skiers—a derring-do snow sport we never dreamed of when I learned to ski.

My first taste of skiing had been in 1945 at a similar so-called mountain near Ishpeming, Michigan, in the iron-ore country of the Upper Peninsula. With mining defunct, the town had been turned into a tourist destination famous for ski jumps, cross-country trails, and the U.S. National Ski Hall of Fame. I was nine, and my parents had taken us for a ski vacation at the historic lodge. Its long hallways and plush carpets remain dreamy in memory, but falling on the bunny slope while trying to master the rope tow is nightmare-vivid.

Here is the drill: the wet rope slips through my grasp, burning a brown indentation into the palms of new ski mittens. When I grab on, the rope jerks me forward. Stiff-legged and bending at the waist, I fall flat on my face. People pile up behind as I lie on my butt, legs up like an overturned crab, struggling to kick long wooden skis out of the way. My father comes to the rescue but puts me back in the metaphorical saddle. This happens again and again until I figure out how to bend my knees, loosen my grip, and let the rope pull me up the hill.

Forty years after my first lessons in skiing, I drove toward Marquette with Bill, passing through Ishpeming. I wanted to show him the place where I had been initiated into snow sports, but compared to our Rocky Mountains, the hills in northern Michigan seemed no more than an outbreak of pimples, and we drove right by without noticing the ski hill. Nevertheless, to the pig-tailed nine-year-old in heavy wooden skis with bear-claw bindings, Ishpeming's slope was plenty high. Luckily, once I reached the top of the hill, my father taught me to fall, to get up by myself, and to leave a trail of V's as I snowplowed down the slope.

I have enjoyed skiing downhill and cross-country ever since, although never as elegantly as Kathy or as hotshot as Carole, which leads me to wonder why I was such an awkward girl. My lack of coordination could have been a relic of polio, or not, but no matter the cause, I remained clumsy and self-conscious when it came to moving my body, and my efforts at learning ballet turned out to be as much of a wreck as learning to ride the rope tow.

At eleven and a half, I was large for my age, developing breasts, already menstruating, and taking ballet lessons with Kathy at the Fine Arts Building in Chicago. At the end of a series of lessons, I overheard our teacher talking to my mother. "Yes, Kathy is doing very well," she said. "She will be a dancer if she keeps on practicing. But it's no use with Annick. She does not have talent. And did you know she has B.O.? It's not pleasant to have her in class."

Talk about humiliation! No wonder I immersed myself in books. It didn't take coordination to read a book. Or write a book. And you could be by yourself while doing it! I could swim before I turned five and have hiked all my life, but it took years of being drilled by Dave to learn to throw a ball and hit a ball well enough to play co-rec softball in my thirties, and more years being coached by Bill to play golf in my fifties. Ten years practicing yoga in my sixties and seventies have at last allowed me to feel confident that my body will do what I tell it to do. But now, as fate will have it, just as I gain balance, my limbs and back are losing the battle with age and arthritis.

A wet pinkish-brown nose breaks my reverie. Bruno circles behind me in his auto-lair. We have arrived at a high-end development called the Eagle Ridge Golf Resort and Spa. Bill loves to investigate new golf courses—something he would do with Pat, but nothing I would do on my own. Now he and Pat seem to be riding shotgun. Pat whispers, "Turn here." Bill says, "Stop!" I hate backseat drivers but cannot resist those big guys.

"Your time has come," I tell Brunie. He eyes me quizzically. Manicured greens meld into a view of forested ridges skirting the Mississippi Valley. Brunie leaps from the car. We would like to take a good walk, but there is no path except the golf-cart path, so after he relieves himself we climb back into the SUV and head for Galena, where I hope to find a gas station toilet.

The city is older and more gracious than I imagined. Built on hills sloping toward the riverfront, its red-brick downtown invites me to shop for antiques, or at least have a cappuccino and croissant as well as a rest stop. I pull into a parking space across from City Hall and haul out my Illinois map of historic places. I learn the city was home to Ulysses S. Grant, who came to Galena in 1860 after retiring from an army career. He worked in his family's leather goods store and then signed up as a volunteer officer in the Union Army. The rest is legend.

Herman Melville also lived in Galena. Like Grant, he came looking for work. He stayed with his uncle during the 1840s, but found no job in the lead mines and went back to New England to seek his fortunes on a whaler at sea. I wonder what Melville would have written had he gone underground in the Driftless Zone.

Heartland Motel. Bruno and I cross the Mississippi at Dubuque and motor onto Iowa's fertile glaciated plains. Once, big bluestem and Indian grasses rose ten feet tall on these prairies and sheltered deer and cougars, bison and wolves. A man on horseback had to stand up in his stirrups to see where he was going. Now the tall grasses have been tamed to corn and wheat, and what wildness remains may be found in tornados, blizzards, bars, meth labs, revival meetings, and far-right politics.

Highway 20 shoots us west onto higher ground, and as the sun lowers to a horizon as flat as the sea's, I begin to look for shelter. Near Waterloo and Cedar Rapids, I spot a billboard for a motel called Heartland. Heartland! I have no choice but to go there. The place is a two-story brick building with white columns, surrounded by vacant lots in a town notable for its meatpacking and food-processing plants, a John Deere tractor factory, Bosnian refugees, and the University of Northern Iowa.

The Heartland's lobby is redolent with popping corn and chocolate chip cookies. I stuff a warm cookie into my mouth and ask if I can bring my dog. "We don't allow pets," says the bored girl at the desk. "But I think there's one room you can stay in."

Our ground-floor room stinks like an ashtray full of butts. Stale smoke permeates the wallpaper and inhabits the thin carpet. I was a smoker for thirty years and will occasionally give in to the comfort a cigarette offers an addict, but a room like this makes me glad to be a quitter. As I open the windows to let in some fresh air, I wonder if the proprietor thinks dog stink and smoke stink are the same.

Next morning in the sunlit breakfast room, I find myself surrounded by fat old people and fat middle-age people and fat young people and fat kids. Like me, they are indulging in the Heartland's carbo-loaded free breakfasts: cereal, bagels, doughnuts, yogurt, fruit, and Belgian waffles soaked in butter and syrup. This is the first time I have seen do-it-yourself waffles in a motel, but it will not be my last. A plump boy with fair hair cut short around his ears makes three golden-brown servings, handing one after another to his beefy dad. My mouth is watering. I love waffles.

Waterloo is not the only place across the plains where I will be struck by the girth of locals and travelers. I was astonished yesterday to see an extra-large woman at a gas station convenience store order a gallon of root beer and, with her Pekinese clutched under one arm, toddle off to her sedan sipping at her straw. As I travel cross-country I will continue to see doughnut eaters and burger and fries eaters, beer drinkers, and super-sizers putting grub away as if this were their last meal.

The heartland's epidemic of gluttony is a problem of poverty and big-ag public policy as much as a question of taste and hunger. Humans have always loved sweets, but our lobby-bullied government is largely to blame for health-destroying excess. It subsidizes the growing of corn—most of it in the heartland—and the processing of corn syrup. Our taxes pay farmers to sell corn cheap to corporations such as Coca-Cola, and though it's healthier to buy organic vegetables or a lean steak, the cost is higher and the pleasure lower. For a couple of dollars a shopper like me might buy healthy food totaling 250 calories, while the same two bucks buys a poorer and hungrier shopper 2,500 calories of satisfaction in a corn-syrup product.

Others more qualified have written books and made movies about this conundrum. Still, I cannot stop wondering about the hunger that drives people to super-size. In frontier mythologies that my generation was taught to revere, the national hunger was for land. The goal was to feed, not to consume. Our image of quintessential America was the breadbasket prairie. Its people were white, Protestant, and agricultural. Also stoic, acquisitive, hardworking, and self-reliant. They lived on family farms, tilled a Jeffersonian dreamland, and were protected by lawmen modeled on the righteous and violent horseback heroes of westerns. Although reality has moved to agribusiness, Mexican field-workers, and surveillance cameras, the myth survives in conservative politics and heartland anger. Especially among people of my generation.

The identity myth of settlement attracted me deeply when I was growing up because it was so different from my urban life, and because it was filled with the beauties of open spaces and horses—denoting freedom. It did not tell me that most settlers were immigrants like my family: Czechs or Swedes or southern blacks or displaced Native Americans. And it implied a superior white-bread brand that I found to be real and repulsive.

For as long as I can remember, my parents would take us girls to Chicago's Art Institute to immerse us in art—especially the impressionists and modernists. On our way back from those galleries we lingered among American paintings of the thirties and forties, some by artists who were friends of my father. I remember standing in front of Grant Wood's *American Gothic*—a farmer holding a pitchfork, his daughter (or was it his wife?) sexless with her hair in a bun and a cameo brooch at her buttoned-up throat. A white farmhouse looms churchlike in the background, complete with its gothic window. The composition is rigid, as are the people.

I did not know until much later that Wood was from Iowa and gay, and that the farmer's daughter was his sister Nan. Or that he was trying to transpose the flat, frontal northern Renaissance style onto the rural Midwest. And I had no inkling the painting was satiric. What I knew was this picture had nothing to do with me. I could imagine myself among Renoir's riverboat revelers, or taking a Degas bath, or kicking up my legs in a Toulouse-Lautrec dance hall. I felt familiar with Cézanne's apples and Ben Shan's brick cityscapes. Van Gogh's delirious night skies caused me to shiver with longings, but I never felt kinship with those Calvinist farmers.

Forty years after settling with my family on a quarter-section of Montana meadow, I am able to identify with the lives of farmers and ranchers, although not entirely. Our family has raised chickens, owned horses, leased our land to run cattle, and planted gardens, but in a hobby-farmer way. The ranchers who are my neighbors tend animals and grow crops for a living, albeit such a meager living that most have jobs in town or at the mill, logging the woods or cleaning houses. That stoic *American Gothic* look has to do with facing up to drought and blizzards, plagues of grasshoppers, the physical labor of tending animals. And yet the ranchers I know tell jokes, like to tease, and drink a beer or two. Their faces are alive and ruddy, and their lives more surprising and enigmatic than the myth would have us believe.

When I was a child, America was 70 percent rural and 30 percent urban. Now the opposite is true. Myth be damned, we are a country of city dwellers. This plains Waterloo is an industrial city. It has a substantial black population, some Indians, a growing Hispanic community, a portion of WASPs from the farms, and the refugee Bosnians. The mix is our new heartland. It exists in Sioux City, Council Bluffs, Omaha, Pierre, Bismarck, and Billings. American gothic has given way to urban diversity, but Tea Party libertarians and traditional conservatives—mostly middle-aged, white, male, and well off—still hold to the frontier myth of conquest and racial superiority. It will be their identity until death. And then, hopefully, it will be gone.

Chautauqua. May 24. Continuing on Highway 20, Bruno and I traverse miles of pastureland, slow down in tree-shaded towns, take a detour in Grundy County where a freeway is being built across some farmer's cornfield. I tune the radio to country-and-western stations but find no emergent Hank Williams. I wish I had another novel on tape. Bill calls on my cell phone. The loneliness of his voice is a poke to my ribs; then it's lost in a hiss of static. As we approach Fort Dodge he gets through long enough to tell me that tomorrow Steve will be cooking up a salmon feed at the ranch for Pat's son Chris and his wife, Rhonda. They have come from Portland to pick up Pat's possessions and his ashes, to empty the apartment and settle his estate.

"Not much of an estate," I quip. "Pat could carry all his stuff in his old Honda."

"We're expecting you to be there."

"I'll try," I say.

I am relieved that my Good Samaritan Steve has taken charge. He will be barbequing the salmon he caught in Idaho. He knows that nurturing mourners is the proper way to stave off the loneliness of a death in the family.

"We'll wait for you."

"No. Don't wait. I'm going as fast as I can."

"Good," says Bill. "Go faster."

At seventy miles per hour, I'm above the speed limit on this two-lane, passing Sunday churchgoers in Pontiacs and barreling around pickups with dogs in the back and watching for cops. I push down on the gas pedal, and the speedometer climbs to eighty. Flags are flying in every small town along our route. In the old river town of Sac City the broad lawn fronting the red-brick city hall is a forest of Stars and Stripes. Passing cemeteries cut off from fields by high iron fences, I notice people in bunches bearing flowers. Memorial Day is tomorrow.

We've been driving nonstop for hours. My rear end is sore. Bruno looks at me hopefully. "You're in luck, buddy," I tell him.

On the outskirts of Sac City is a park with grass clearings, clumps of willow trees, and a green river called Raccoon. I park by the river. Bruno stretches in the yoga pose called downward-facing dog. He stands in his look-before-you-leap posture, then leaps into the river. I stretch, too, bending to the left and to the right. I touch my toes. Raise my arms over my head. Take a long inhale and a long exhale. This is time out for both of us. Brunie's wet coat gleams red in the sunlight. He sheds water, spraying my pants, but I don't mind. Both of us are content with the dance of stream and scent of willows.

We stroll toward an octagonal white building set in a sweep of lawn. I see screened porches surrounding large glassed-in rooms. A sign painted above the porch reads "Chautauqua Bldg, 1908." I try to imagine the 1908 chautauqua. My mother was two that year. She lived in Transylvania (now Romania) in a town called Nagyvárad (now Oradea) at the edge of the Hungarian *puszta*. Her town was much larger than Sac City and centuries older, dominated by a ruined Turkish castle on the hill. But there, as here, in 1908, the square would be crowded with horse-drawn buggies. Farmers' wagons would be coming to market. A few of the earliest motor cars might show off on the central boulevard. And my grandfather and grandmother Beck would be promenading the *corso*, him in a straw boater, her in a Gibson Girl dress.

They'd hold tight to their son Jean's small hand and would be showing off little Ilonka (Helenc) in her frills and bows.

If I live nearly one hundred years, as Mom has done, I wonder if this chautauqua building will still be standing. And I wonder how much change a person can experience and not go batshit. Chautauquas were institutions of the heartland: democratic, cultural—everyone was invited. There would be band concerts and theatricals and lectures, puppet shows, magic acts, and minstrels.

I peer through the old building's screened porch. It looks as if it is still in use. What acts will chautauqua bring to Sac City this year? Across the United States in towns like Sac City or Missoula as well as in cities such as Los Angeles and New York, the spirit of chautauqua lives on in film festivals and bluegrass festivals and choral festivals and book fairs—Carnivale in San Francisco; South by Southwest in Austin; Santa Barbara's film festival; Shakespeare in a Brooklyn park; rock concerts in eastern Washington's Columbia Gorge; Burning Man in Nevada's Black Rock Desert; Missoula's annual Book Fair. It's gratifying to know that in the age of television, Facebook, and Twitter, we still like to gather face to face. We get high on music or words or wine or weed. We become giddy with the perfumes of strangers.

Across the 100th Meridian. For lunch I order a sloppy "southwestern" salad at a Chili's restaurant on the Nebraska side of Sioux City. Afterward, along the dust-blown main drag, I pass Mexican restaurants, markets, and small businesses. I'd have fared better in one of those beaneries, but I did not expect such an influx of Mexicans. It confirms what I discovered in Waterloo. White folks may rule the plains, but the workers who cultivate and harvest our corn and grain are mostly brown.

The black-haired children hopping around their mothers like baby birds were born in America. Immigrants, legal or illegal, are once again populating the plains. It's a cleaving issue in this early caucus state where presidential candidates are chosen. The subject of immigration divides racists from opportunists, white business folk who need cheap labor from white folk afraid of losing their privileges. No matter. The immigrants are here. Soon it will be their turn to be in charge.

At Royal, we drive by the Northeast Nebraska Zoo and though I am curious to see what manner of beasts might be found there, I do not slow down. Highway 20 veers north along the Elkhorn River, and tilled fields give way to grass. We are some fifty miles east of the 100th meridian, which marks the official division between the moist tallgrass prairies of the Midwest and the more arid mid- and short-grass plains of the West. I feel the change as well as see it when we pass through O'Neill. Ranches have replaced farmsteads. Cattle graze the prairies. As the land rises, opens, and empties, I am filled with a surge of happiness—a westerner running toward home.

One of the joys of driving with dogs is the imperative to stop every few hours and relieve ourselves of the pressures of bladder and confinement and, for me at least, of the dual foci of road and memory. I turn onto a gravel ranch track that parallels the river (Bruno and I will always choose a river if one is available). I look for wildflowers. Bruno scares up a grouse in a thicket and, excited as only a bird dog can be, runs a zigzag line retracing its scent path. A red-tailed hawk circles above. The blue of sky is more translucent here. Lighter in density. I take deep breaths. Hello. Oh yes! The air is invigorating, breezy, sweet.

We cross the invisible 100th meridian at a hamlet called Johnstown and say howdy to Mountain Time. There are no mountains on any horizon, but we have driven into the rain shadow of the Rockies. I will not realize until I study the map this evening that this Elkhorn section of Highway 20 is itself a divide. To the north lie the Great Plains and Indian country, but south and west, underpinning rolling formations undistinguishable to my untrained eye, are the geologically and ecologically unique nineteen thousand square miles of grass-covered dunes called the Sandhills. Almost undisturbed now, except by grazing cattle, I cannot know that in a few years these green prairies will be a battleground for those who want to drill down to the rock-bound oil beneath its grasslands or run a giant pipeline through it, endangering the great Ogallala Aquifer, which is the major source of water for ranchers and farmers and all the towns and reservations that inhabit these wide-open spaces.

Valentine. Bill calls as we approach Valentine. Perfect timing, for this is one of his favorite watering holes. A few years ago he drove the 100th meridian from Canada to Mexico to research an essay for a book of photographs. It was a long ride across barren country and skeleton towns, and Valentine was a pleasant surprise. Our friend Jim Harrison is a connoisseur of the Nebraska heartlands and also favors Valentine.

"There's a decent bookstore," Bill tells me, bookstores being his marker of a civilized place. And restaurants featuring marbled Nebraska steaks tender as butter, which he does not like "too mushy." Motels and bed and breakfasts abound, also sporting goods and tourist shops. These riches are in Valentine because the Niobrara River runs through it, a National Scenic River with sandstone gorges and ninety-three waterfalls and world-class canoeing, rafting, and kayaking. Game preserves and bike trails attract bird-watchers and exercise addicts. There are rodeos in summer and access to the Sioux tribes of the nearby Rosebud Reservation. I detour through town, giving Bill a blow-by-blow description and knowing that what I say is not what matters. The touch of a beloved voice is the solace he craves.

I think of our friend Gretel Ehrlich and her book *The Solace of Open Spaces.* For me, as for her, respite from loss can be found in the sweep of sagebrush, the ocean's roar, the cracking of Arctic ice. Or down in the Grand Canyon whose layers of red, lavender, and yellow rock remind us that human existence is but a thin striation in the drifts of time. There is solace, too, in the transient beauties of birdsong. Deep inside canyons the canyon wren sings. And on the plains, the meadowlark. But for Bill, who grew up on a high plains ranch miles from any town, where interior monologues were the most available source of communication, solace is having someone to talk to.

Talking about Valentine is a relief from talking about Pat, but Pat is always on our minds. "I went to Pat's apartment with Chris and Rhonda," says Bill, "to dig through his stuff. I took a couple of things—a golf club I gave him—a couple of books. We packed most of it up for the Salvation Army, but not Patty's collection of golf caps."

Chris will carry the caps back to Portland—his father's *memento mori*—and weeks later he will telephone Bill to report that while sorting through the hats he noticed one that was heavier than the others. Inside its sweatband he found $1,600 in small bills. Pat's nest egg. I can almost see Pat returning from his night shift pale and hunched with fatigue. He opens his closet, rifles through his pants pockets and stashes a few bucks from his paycheck into that hat—way back in a corner on a high shelf. Is the hat red, or blue? Ragged and stained or brand-new? No matter. This will be his secret cache, as private and hidden as he is—and safe from the clutches of the IRS.

"It's a great day for the Memorial Day tournament," says Bill, but he will not be competing today. Golf has been his obsession since he began caddying as a kid in Lakeview, Oregon—a distraction from ranch work and a way to escape its isolation. Now it's his old-man escape from the sedentary life of ideas and imagination. Bill taught creative writing at the University of Montana for twenty-nine years. Teaching kept him occupied, but writing has been the core of his life since he left the ranch at age thirty-five.

Writing, however, takes only part of each day. "Golf is something to do in the afternoons," Bill laughs. And golf is far healthier than drinking—the other writer's sport he indulged in all over the West, a habit of his generation that would help kill off most of his close friends: Ray Carver, Dick Hugo, Max Crawford, Jim Welch, and even the seemingly bulletproof Jim Crumley.

"I've got no one my age to talk to anymore," Bill complains. He is thinking of Pat, who was a golfer and a drinker and a brotherly confidant, and his other lost cronies.

"What about me?" I counter. Of course Bill talks to me, but a gal doesn't count the same as guys in this game. "What are you doing tonight?" I ask, hoping he will not get drunk with his younger pals at the Depot Bar and Grill.

Booze, I know from experience, does not mix with grief. You're going for dissociation of the senses and what you get is heightened emotion. Tides of grief break out of control before the last good drink brings on the nothingness of passing out. "I'm taking Chris and Rhonda to the Depot for dinner."

Good, I think. Drinking will happen. But so will eating. Being with family at crisis time, no matter how tenuous the connection, is usually the best idea.

Rest Stop. Soon I am out of Valentine and Bill is out of cell-phone range. I have been so involved with driving and talking that I forgot to stop for gas. The 4Runner devours gas like the hog it is, and I have never tested how far the near-empty tank will take me. The sun is dropping, dusk approaching, and here I am on an empty highway in an empty land, no gas station for miles.

At Cody, Nebraska, I think we may have some gas station luck, but all I see in the one-street false-front town is a gathering of horse trailers, a few kids on horseback, and banners announcing tomorrow's Memorial Day Rodeo. I head for Merriman some twenty miles west and make it. With my tank full, my stomach unknots and I look for a place to walk with Bruno. We had passed a turnoff to the Cottonwood Lakes Recreation area a few miles back. The spot looked promising. Bruno is crunched under the open back window at the farthest end of the SUV with his head between his paws. His eyes are half-shut. I am saddened by his stillness. There is something heart-wrenching in the implacable resignation of dogs.

"Buddy," I say, "you deserve a swim." He remains rock still. A wee twitch at the tip of his tail tells me he has heard and approves.

The oval lake sits in a depression among low green-thatched dunes and is fringed with cottonwoods and marsh grasses. I park near a camping area where several pickups with campers and trailers have set up for the night. Picnic tables are piled with chips and beer. Someone has lighted a charcoal grill. A couple of boys are playing ball. Two people paddle a canoe across pewter waters. A man in silhouette fishes from a rowboat. Bruno trots toward shore and stops at attention. Then, inevitable as the setting sun, he plunges in.

The tops of scattered cottonwoods are gilded, but the shore is shadowed black. The hum of insects, a splash of oars, murmurs of distant voices accentuate the prairie's serenity, but serenity is broken by a grizzled man in a white T-shirt and overalls—maybe drunk, maybe simply violent and angry—who shouts at a tiny girl. The girl cowers. The man approaches her, hand raised. The girl begins to cry. A heavy-set woman in shorts grabs the child and pulls her into the trailer. I'd like to confront the brutish man, but know better. There can be no happy ending.

Old Jules. Driving toward Chadron, I face a circle of blinding light. I move slowly toward the glare, squinting despite sun-glasses, and thankful the highway is as deserted as the grasslands it cuts through. At last the haze that masks the horizon swallows the sun. What remains is a purplish band outlined in glittering orange. The land darkens. Driving becomes automatic and my mind turns inward.

My first sight of this country was in June 1978. I'd flown to Scottsbluff, Nebraska, rented a car, and headed east into the Sandhills. My mission was to delve into the place and family that had inspired the Nebraska writer Mari Sandoz. Our Wilderness Women production company in Missoula had decided to film Elinore Stewart's Wyoming homesteader story (the film that would become *Heartland*) as the pilot for a projected series, and we were looking for the next good frontier woman's tale to follow it into production. I knew something of Mari's history but had only book learning about the place that sparked her imagination. If I were to write a script about her life, I had to put my feet on her ground.

Mari was born in 1896 in her father's Post Office shack overlooking the Niobrara River. The eldest of six children—and by rules of female primogeniture, the nursemaid for the rest—she grew up on homesteads hidden in the grassland swells that I am passing through now. Her father, Jules Sandoz, became both famous and infamous through her unflinchingly candid portrayal of him in her 1935 memoir, *Old Jules,* one of the great narratives of the pioneer West.

On his deathbed, Jules surprised Mari by asking her to write his life story. It was an odd request, as he had never encouraged her before. In fact, when she published her first short story at age eleven, he had slapped her face and locked her in the cellar.

"Fiction," Jules shouted, "is only fit for hired girls."

Years later he told her, "You know I consider artists and writers the maggots of society." But as he lay dying, he realized that his only passage to immortality would be through the words of his writer daughter.

Jules Sandoz had emigrated to the prairies from Switzerland with dreams of Utopian settlements, orchards, and forests. He was an educated man but a self-taught homesteader: grumpy, prideful, eccentric, often failing in his ambitions, and yet a champion of the small farmer rather than the big rancher. Jules was a nurturer of trees and a destroyer of women. His violent temper and negligence helped drive his first wife, a Swiss immigrant named Henriette, to divorce and madness.

Madness was not uncommon in female homesteaders. In winter the empty prairies were (and still are) brutally cold; in summer, drought seared the grasslands, and grasshoppers gobbled the crops. Blizzards and firestorms, nonstop labor, absent husbands, no nearby relatives or neighbors, and a constant wind might make anyone hide in the root cellar. In Henriette's case, Jules's abuse became unbearable, and she fled from him, lived in a cave, and ultimately died in an insane asylum.

After Henriette divorced him, Jules ordered up a second wife. This was Mary Sandoz, known as Marlizzie, the mother of Mari and her five siblings. Mary was a mail-order bride from Germany—a small, delicate, and stylish woman. When she descended from the stagecoach to meet her husband to be, she carried a suitcase packed with eight new dresses of cashmere and twill and figured French serge. On Jules's homestead, thirty miles from the nearest railroad, with only a few far-off neighbors, Marlizzie had no occasion to wear such finery. So she cut up her dresses into clothes for her children—all six born in a shack with no doctor in attendance. Then, after Jules died, with her children grown and gone, Mary took over the home place.

In her late, autobiographical book, *Sandhill Sundays*, Mari would describe her mother with the grace begotten by love:

> You will find her away somewhere chasing a turkey hen, looking
> after the cattle, repairing fence with stretchers and staples. . . .
> She comes smiling and curious. . . . And as she approaches, you
> see her wonderful wiry slightliness, notice that her forearms,
> always bare, are like steel with twisted cables under dark leather—
> with hands that are beautiful in the knotted vigor that has
> gripped the hoe and the pitchfork until the fingers can never be

straightened, fingers that still mix the ingredients for the world's most divine concoction—Swiss plum pie."

Plum pies or no, it did not surprise me that Mari's mother experienced abandonment and despair, felt fury toward her husband, and had once attempted suicide. "Don't marry an Old Country man," Marlizzie warned her daughters, "or you'll be a slave."

Mari Sandoz escaped her father's orbit as soon as she could, only to fall into a similar trap. At seventeen, with only an eighth-grade education, she became a country schoolteacher. A year later she married a neighboring rancher, and at twenty-three, divorced him for "extreme mental cruelty." Then she fled to Lincoln, Nebraska, where she wrote constantly, lived in poverty, attended classes at the University of Nebraska, and suffered the predictable failures of a woman writer from the backcountry. Her breakthrough book, *Old Jules*, was rejected by thirteen publishers before a revised version won a prize from the *Atlantic* and was published in 1935. Its success enabled her to move to Denver, and then to New York. She settled in Greenwich Village, where she enjoyed the Bohemian pleasures of a city woman, the discipline of a researcher, and the satisfactions of a writer who published more than twenty books, including *Cheyenne Autumn*, *Crazy Horse*, and *The Cattlemen*. She never married again, had no children, and died of bone cancer in 1966. But like many western-bred artists who grew up in rural isolation, poverty, or both—like friends of mine such as Judy Blunt, Mary Blew, Bill Kittredge, James Welch, and Richard Hugo—Mari Sandoz's imagination resided in the home that drove her away.

"Through discovery of this region," she wrote of the Sandhills, "this one drop of water, I hope to discover something of the nature of the ocean."

Young Jules. A green-black gloom settles over the Sandhills. I look north toward darkening grasslands, and my thoughts turn from Mari to her younger brother, known as Young Jules. It was a lucky day when I met him about twenty-five years ago, the day I first drove into these Sandhills. I catch my breath realizing how fast a quarter of a century slips by, and yet his presence is imprinted in my memory as it is on this landscape.

The afternoon was breezy, with tawny-topped grasses swaying under a June sun. Grazed dunes dipped and swelled around me. The land was barren of trees or any break from the blue horizontal save for an occasional shack or windmill. I parked at a crossroads where the blacktop met up with a dirt track. A tall, thin old cowboy eased out of a maroon 1960s vintage Mercury. This was Young Jules, square-jawed, blue-eyed, and courtly in pressed Levi's, polished cowboy boots, and a straw Stetson. He had come to lead me to his sister's ranch.

"No telling where you'd end up," he said, sizing me up as a dude. Jules opened the door on the passenger side and we took off in his rattling rig, careening almost airborne on dusty ranch roads at speeds no sane person would dare.

Still handsome at eighty, Young Jules glanced sideways at me from time to time, a naughty half-smile daring me to flinch. I held tight, knowing this was a test. He slowed down once to point out Mari's grave. Further on, he nodded at a fork in the road. "That's the way to the home place. We'll go there tomorrow."

We pulled into Caroline Sandoz Pifer's driveway in a spatter of dust and gravel. The youngest Sandoz sister lived with her husband in a neat, sixties-style two-level ranch house with picture windows looking out to the open pastures of their ranch. The house was decorated western style with braided rugs, cowboy art, potted plants, and maple furniture. Family photos hung in the hallway along with a few of Mari's artifacts and honors. There was a border collie in the yard, and a tabby cat in the kitchen. At least that's the picture in my mind.

Caroline was a trim, well-spoken woman and a gracious host, but hesitant about spilling any more family secrets than Mari had revealed in her books. For instance, she didn't tell me the Sandoz children grew up speaking German. Or that, to hold his claim under the Kinkaid Act, Old Jules had sent fourteen-year-old Mari and ten-year-old Young Jules to camp on a homestead miles away for four months, expecting them to survive on what they could scrounge. But she did quiz me about our small corporation's plans for a movie.

The film my partners and I had in mind, I told her, would not be a celebrity story about Mari or a biography of Old Jules. It would be based on the life of their mother, Marlizzie—her experiences as an immigrant mail-order bride and then as a mother of six who managed the family ranch with little help from her husband. The movie we wanted to make would not be about an exceptional woman who got away but about a woman who held her ground.

Caroline was evasive. Other producers had been in touch with the family about television or movie projects based on Mari's life and books. I inferred from her tone that she believed those others had deeper pockets, better connections, and more likely chances for success than a group called Wilderness Women from Missoula, Montana. "We'll talk about it and I'll get back to you," she said. I knew she never would.

Young Jules joked and laughed as he drove me to the home place next morning. The ranch had gone to his sister Flora. In overalls and work boots, with cropped gray hair and a strong, stout body, Flora was the frontier woman I had expected Caroline to be. She nodded politely when Jules told her I wanted to make a movie about her mother. I talked about our plan to depict as honestly as we could the lives of homestead women, but I don't think she believed me. How could this frizzy haired, obviously urban woman in jeans and polished boots have the faintest notion about her mother's character or life?

Flora showed me around the barn and chicken coop and pointed out a few old apple trees that Jules had planted, as well as some struggling cottonwoods. "Trees," she said. "He wanted to plant trees out here."

On our way back to my rental car, Young Jules drove more slowly. He quizzed me about my life in Montana, my sons, my status as a widow. He was flirtatious and charming—disappointed when I told him I had a steady boyfriend.

"Watch out for Jules," Caroline had advised before we left her place that morning. "He likes you!" Then, with a softening of voice and a concerned wrinkling of her forehead, she added, "You know he has cancer. Incurable. He don't show it, but he's eighty— a very sick man."

When we arrived at the crossroads, Jules stopped the car but did not get out. He leaned toward me, grabbed my shoulders, and planted a big kiss on my lips.

"What the hell . . . ?" I laughed. He laughed. Then he opened his door and came round to escort me toward my vehicle. After I was in the driver's seat, my bag stowed in the trunk, my briefcase beside me, Young Jules stood a moment looking down at me. He tipped his Stetson.

"Now," he said, "you can tell those folks in Montana you been kissed by a real cowboy!"

The Last Best Place. It is near dark when we arrive in Chadron. A place of convergences. Deep in the prairie heart of Sioux country, this is the West of western movies. When I was a child in Chicago, I lost myself in Sunday matinees at the Clark Theatre. I loved those cowboys. Loved the Indians. Especially loved the horses. In my fantasies, when I wasn't Wonder Woman with her invisible helicopter, I was an Indian maiden riding a silver-blue stallion. My black hair streamed from under a headband decorated with a single eagle feather. The wild herd ran behind, enveloped in red dust.

As a devotee of storytelling, I believe "we are what we daydream." A westerner for more than half a century, I have schooled myself in western history, and the most compelling stories I found are, like Marlizzie's, about *survival* rather than *conquest*. My primary education took place during four years in the 1980s when Bill Kittredge and I, along with writers and historians James Welch, Mary Clearman Blew, Bill Bevis, Bill Lang, and Richard Roeder, gathered reams of material for an anthology of Montana writings that we edited for the state's centennial. Our subjects ranged from Indian oral tales through Lewis and Clark to homesteader narratives. And we included fiction by Montana writers Dorothy Johnson, A.B. Guthrie Jr., and Norman Maclean, as well as the poems of Richard Hugo.

Like Paris, like Greenwich Village, like Jackson, Mississippi, the State of Montana was and continues to be a storied place that invites storytellers. Our thousand-plus-page volume was titled *The Last Best Place*—a name Bill coined and a phrase that would become a state slogan on license plates and the logo of our Republican senator's stationery. An inverted version became the name of a cemetery called the Best Last Place.

To our immense surprise our oversize volume became a model for regional anthologies, a benchmark book about the American West, and a bestseller distributed far beyond Montana. Once, when Bill and I dropped in at the English-language bookstore Village Books in Paris (now sadly defunct), we found *The Last Best Place* prominently displayed. "Oh yes," said the proprietor. "It is always wanted here."

Like the Montana recorded in *The Last Best Place*, Chadron partakes of all the truths of the Great Plains. In prehistoric times, it was prime bison range for local tribes. By the early 1800s, the Teton Sioux had driven out competitors and claimed the area. Then Spanish fur traders built trading posts and sold hides of bison and game for good profits. They were followed by French and American traders who opened trails across Indian country that were used by wagon trains heading for California or Oregon. The wagon trains were harassed by Indians trying to protect their territory, so U.S. soldiers rode in and built forts to shield them. Then came cattlemen driving herds from Texas. And the bison were wiped out.

Violence between Indians and Anglos increased after the Civil War, when gold was discovered in the Black Hills. Crazy Horse and Sitting Bull won notable battles, which fueled popular support for revenge, conquest, and genocide. By 1877—one year after their victory at the Battle of the Little Bighorn—the U.S. government had enticed most of the Sioux bands onto reservations with promises of food, shelter, and medical care, but the Indians remained starving and in despair.

The Ghost Dance religion brought last-ditch hope while making Indian agents fearful of rebellion. Sitting Bull's slaughter in December 1890 on the Standing Rock Reservation was instigated by agent McLaughlin's fear of the Ghost Dancers. The infamous Massacre at Wounded Knee Creek took place a week or so later, tearing the heart out of Sioux resistance. But even at the brink of eradication, the defeated peoples did not go easy—or go at all. In 1973, at what is called Wounded Knee II, we witnessed the rise of a new American Indian militancy, and the return of government oppression.

Modern Chadron is a border town with built-in conflicts. Still-contested Sioux lands in the Black Hills channel tourists as they once attracted gold diggers. Wounded Knee has become a shrine, while the Pine Ridge Reservation remains one of the most poverty-stricken pockets in America. Chadron State College has created a Mari Sandoz Heritage Center in the old library where Mari once studied; and on the plains, bison in small clusters have been restored to native lands.

I drive up Main Street past historic brick buildings and Victorian mansions to a Spanish-style Best Western on a hill. The sky is indigo set with stars and lit by a quarter moon. This is the

Sunday of graduation. Partygoers in long dresses and dark suits unload a case of champagne (or is it beer?) in the driveway. The girl at the desk has the high cheekbones of her tribe. She tells me all rooms are taken. I turn away and she takes pity. There is one room remaining. The Jacuzzi suite. I ask if dogs are allowed. "Sure," she says. "I'll give it to you for the price of a regular room."

I lug our gear up a flight of stairs to a two-room suite with a kitchenette and, in the bathroom, a giant bathtub. Bruno is salivating with hunger. After feeding him, I find a McDonald's down the road and devour a double cheeseburger and fries. By the time I get back I'm so tired I don't even try the Jacuzzi.

I dive into the king-sized bed and am drifting into sleep when Brunie yelps in a doggie nightmare, his paws running. I take out my book of dog poems. Leafing through poems about dying dogs and stray dogs or neurotic dogs, I have a hard time settling on one that will help me and Bruno go back to sleep. We are in Indian country, so I pick a Pima poem called "Dog Song," told in part from a dog's point of view:

> Our songs begin at nightfall
> when the wind blows from the south—
> the wind is strong,
> bending my tail toward the north.
> Butterfly wings begin to fall.
> Butterfly wings are falling
> that hurt me when they fall . . .
> *See the little dogs come running!*
> *See the poor dogs come running!*
> *See the horsemen coming after,*
> *see the horsemen come laughing!*

"Dream of the horsemen," I tell Bruno, "not the hurting butter-flies." He rests his head on my thigh. I tickle his brown-gold ears. "You can run with them. Look. The dogs are laughing, too!"

HOME

DAY FIFTEEN, MAY 25

Custer State Park. May 25. Today is our last day on the road, and I don't want this trip to end in the sad way it's bound to. I consider veering north toward the Rockies of Alberta, or south to the red deserts of the Colorado Plateau. Bruno and I might head for Santa Fe, then dip down into the Grand Canyon. We might go to Seattle, cross the sound on a ferry and drive to continent's end on the Olympic Peninsula. But no. I can't escape.

Bruno and I take off early on Highway 385 going north toward the Black Hills. Up the road is Hot Springs, famous for its mineral baths and fossilized wooly mammoths, but we don't have time to stop for tourist attractions. I turn onto Route 87, ascending through hilly country toward Wind Cave National Park, whose caverns were mythologized in Sioux legends long before Theodore Roosevelt created the park in 1902. Early explorers reported being frightened by sounds of deep breathing in the night, as if a giant slept below the earth, but I don't stop to put my ear to the limestone, tempting as wind caves might be. We pass bison grazing along the roadside, and I remember they belong to one of the few genetically pure herds in the United States—stock that has been transplanted to the American Prairie Preserve in Montana instead of more common mixed breeds that are part bison, part cattle.

In this high country, spring green and fragrant with pine, we arrive at the first mountain range I have been in for, it seems, half a lifetime. Home, I think. Home at last. I remind myself I've been gone only a couple of weeks. Funny how a girl from the Midwest feels at home in the Rockies and not in her place of rearing. Home, I guess, is a construct of the soul, a recognition more than a history.

I yearn for a break from endless asphalt, so I turn off the pavement into Custer State Park and find a trailhead going down a gentle canyon along French Creek. I let Bruno off his leash and both of us almost skip for joy (if you can imagine a dog skipping) as we skirt the meandering creek through lupine and shooting stars, bluebells, Indian paintbrush, penstemon, and sego lilies. Whitetail deer flit ghostlike in brush and pines, but Bruno is not a deer-chasing dog. I pick wild strawberries and toss him a few.

My internal time clock begins its alarm. Time to go. Reluctantly, Bruno and I retrace our path up the trail. We mount the 4Runner and settle in for the long haul. Soon, we are out of the Black Hills and riding Wyoming's high plains. At Moorcroft I enter the freeway with a sense of defeat. No more backroads for us. It'll be four-lanes all the way home.

Singing the Blues. Bored with my new CDs, I resort to old favorites—Coleman Hawkins, John Coltrane, Louis Armstrong, Ella Fitzgerald, and my chosen soul sister, Billie Holiday. I will never sing the blues like Billie or live the desperate bluesy life she lived, but the yearning comes up in my throat like a swaddled bird, and I wish it could fly.

Music is not my métier no matter how I love it. I had no idea that I was tone-deaf until third grade. That winter, practicing carols with classmates for our Christmas concert, I sang with enthusiasm, loud and off-key, having memorized the words of every carol. A few days before the concert, dour Miss Challacomb pointed her long finger at me. "Anne-*ick*," she said, mispronouncing my name with a nasal Chicago drawl, "from now on, I want you to mouth the words, but don't make a sound." I turned red. Blinked hard to keep back the tears. Felt the eyes of the other kids laughing at me. *A knife to the heart* is a cliché I try to avoid. But that is how I felt. Stabbed. Never again would I sing in public without being self-conscious, but how can a girl give up singing?

Or waltzing in my living room on hardwood floors, alone and swept away with longings. When I'm in dancing mode, a golden oldies radio station playing "Nature Boy" or "Bali Hai" or "Blue Moon" will send me back to the fifties and slow-dancing in some dim, streamer-decked high school gym. Or I'll play records from the sixties that we sang around campfires in Seattle and Montana: Pete Seeger and Woody Guthrie—"Goodnight, Irene" and "When I'm on my journey, don't you weep after me." We bottle-fed our babies on the Beatles. The Kingston Trio. Bob Dylan. In Missoula in the late sixties and seventies, I spent wistful afternoons with Willie Nelson, Bonnie Raitt, Emmylou, and Merle, whose songs can still evoke the whiskey-fed jealousies of a young mother (me) with a husband who has a wandering heart (Dave). And if I'm in a different mood, the same singers and songs will revive the whiskey-fed passions of a young widow (me) being courted by a cowboy version of Dylan Thomas (Bill).

French songs are another story. My mother took my sisters and me to Europe on the great ocean liner *Isle de France* in 1953. The vessel swarmed with French pilots returning home from NATO training in the United States. Talk about girl heaven! My special aviator, Jean-Paul Renaud, was twenty years old, tall, lean, wry, and handsome in a Jimmy Stewart way. We spent the voyage leaning over rails hypnotized by the ever-opening and ever-closing wake, or slow-dancing in the ballroom, or kissing and petting in the dark movie theater. Jean-Paul called me his "leetle, leetle girl," not because I was diminutive but because I was small breasted.

What did I care? We were in love. Ashore, we rendezvoused in Paris where my uncle and aunt lived, and I walked the streets of the nineteenth arrondissement with my aviator, making out under streetlamps along the Canal Saint-Martin as they do in French movies. I planned to run from my family and join him at his base in the south of France. That's how stricken I was. Lucky for us all, Jean-Paul was sent off to Marrakech instead, where I could not follow.

That summer we traded chatty love letters across the Atlantic. And then the letters stopped. His friend Guy, who was Kathy's boy aviator friend, wrote that Jean-Paul had been in an airplane accident and was in the hospital, luckily not fatally injured. After that, my letters to the hospital were returned and Jean-Paul never wrote to me again. I was sure he was dead. Each night back in Wilmette, after my family went to bed, I climbed the narrow stairway to my attic room, took Jean-Paul's letters out of my jewel box, read and reread them until the pale-blue airmail stationery was crumpled and tear-stained. Then I turned on the phonograph. Closing my eyes, I sang *sotto voce* with the sexy melodies of Jacqueline François or wailed with Edith Piaf—singing and weeping into the night.

I cannot imagine doing such things now. At some point a person gets tired of wailing. Maybe what we yearn for—limping oldsters like me—is not lost loves but the return of the heightened emotions of youth. We've lived so many lives and learned so many songs of love and loss that the repetition gets boring. We know our hearts have gotten cooler. But we also know that when they turn pure cold, it will mean that we are dead.

Buffalo Cop. It is blazing noon and I stop at a rest area near Crazy Woman Creek. Bruno and I walk a few moments on a patch of yellowing grass, but it's too hot to dawdle. I fill my water bottle. Pour a dish for Bruno. Memorial Day vacationers fill the car park. We retreat to the air-conditioned peace of the SUV.

The freeway rises and curves through the Bighorns leading up, into, and out of the old cowboy town of Buffalo. This is familiar territory. In the mid-1960s Dave and I horse-packed into the mountains from a dude ranch near Buffalo, bringing Eric and Steve for their first hiking trip. We were led by Carole; her husband, Peter; and his brother, Brad, who had spent summers at that ranch as kids. On the porch of a log bunkhouse, we posed for snapshots. Dave could pass as authentic with his brushy mustache and well-worn straw Stetson. I am definitely a poseur—straddle-legged, with tight jeans tucked *inside* my boots, and my right hand tipping a beat-up felt cowboy hat I found in a second-hand store.

A dozen years later, when Bill and I were driving the West like pilgrims, we became acquainted with every highway, most secondary roads, and quite a few byways from Montana to Arizona and from Wyoming to the Pacific. The Bighorns were one of our routes of passage. We would stop at the crest of Bighorn Canyon to pay our respects at the huge Crow Medicine Ring, a circle of white stones set like a wagon wheel. It is a sacred place, and the fence around it is hung with bundles of feathers, beads, and bright cloths. Then we dropped down to the polo grounds in Story, where nineteenth-century remittance men (aristocratic second sons from Great Britain) played their horse games. Most recently, we were stranded in Sheridan during a January blizzard. Snow swirled so thick we could not see the road, and passing semis buried us in their backwash.

Now I'm drifting along in freeway hypnosis, listening to jazz, and speeding in the fast lane. When I hear a cop's siren, I dutifully slow down and am surprised that his blinking blue light is signaling *me*.

"I clocked you at eighty-seven in a seventy-five-mile zone," says the cop.

The man is old for his job, with a sweating florid face, close-cropped gray hair, and buttons strained around the bulge at his waistline. He looks me over. My long white hair is tied up in a kerchief, I'm braless in a scoop neck T-shirt, and my bare legs seem younger than the rest of me. He grins. Maybe he likes what he sees. I smile back with what I think is a come-on.

"Sorry. Had no idea I was going so fast."

Curious Bruno has come up behind the passenger seat and sticks his nose out the half-open window. The cop studies him a moment.

"Good-lookin' dog. Is he a Chesapeake or a Lab?"

"Chocolate Lab," I say. "His name is Bruno."

The cop reaches out his hand, then pulls it back. "Don't worry," I say. "He's the mellowest dog on record."

The cop pats Bruno on the head and Bruno gives him his dog-smile. If my charms won't work, maybe the dog's will. The cop says he's got an old black female Lab. Would love to have a young buck like Bruno.

"Is he a hunter?" he asks.

"Only when my son takes him grouse hunting."

My good-ole-cop pulls out his ticket pad. Bruno's charms have failed and so have mine. I tell him I'm rushing to Montana because my brother-in-law just died; his relatives are only in town for a couple of days; and I've *got* to meet them before dark. "Wouldn't want you to die gettin' there," he says.

The ticket for going twelve miles over the speed limit is $110. It's useless to argue, so I take the ticket, put on my sunglasses, and pull out into traffic. The cop gets back in his black and white. He's got a Memorial Day quota to fill.

Montana Again. We enter Montana at the border of the Crow Reservation. The cell phone rings. It's Bill. "Will you get here by dinner?"

"Don't think so." Even if I speed at ninety miles per hour, it's still four hundred miles to home. I tell him about my ticket. Can't afford another one. "I'll get there when I get there. Save a piece of salmon."

Bill isn't happy with this news, but there is no way I can helicopter home. When I hit Billings and turn west on I-90, the drive becomes automatic. Here is the Yellowstone River with its cottonwoods and bald eagles; and the ranch town of Big Timber where the cowboy poets gather; and north of it, the Crazy Mountains rearing up in their crazy way. I drive by Livingston, where I could visit Russell Chatham or Doug and Andrea Peacock, or Dave Quammen and stop for a drink and dinner, but I smile and wave. Twenty-five miles down the highway, Bozeman is ringed by fast-food joints and motels, having transformed itself from the slow college town and ski-bum haven it used to be into a place of McMansions and movie star retreats, with developments sprawled across some of the best farmland in the state.

The sun lowers to the west and I pull down my visors. Since this is central Montana, where the law is distant as the horizon, I speed up. At Three Forks, the Jefferson, Madison, and Gallatin rivers join to form the headwaters of the Missouri, and the plains accelerate their upward tilt. We pass Whitehall, where Bill and Dick Hugo got skunked on a fishing trip and ate the best macaroni and cheese ever. Then it's up Pipestone Pass and across the Continental Divide at 6,453 feet, looking out at a sci-fi landscape where scrambled boulders are mixed with brown beetle–killed pines.

I wish I could spend the night at the Finlen Hotel in Butte. I would have a beer and a burger at the M&M Bar and walk the steep mine-drilled neighborhoods. I love Butte. It used to be the industrial, urban center of Montana, but its copper mines are spent and the city is chewed up and spat out, with a poisonous open-pit crater at its center. No matter. Butte is coming back, the locals say, with clean-energy entrepreneurs and cheap housing, while the giant white Virgin of the Rockies blesses the town from her mountaintop.

The 112 miles from Butte to Bonner is a sight of open, cattle-grazed meadows rolling toward blue-tinged mountain ranges from Anaconda through Deer Lodge and past Drummond. As we cross an invisible line, the country narrows into cliffs and canyons, and we enter forested hills and fish-rich river valleys that mark the moister western reaches of this huge state—a state the size of France.

It is nearly eight-thirty when I whiz past the Rock Creek turnoff, and still the sun shines. Dave and I once lived in a rented bungalow at the Valley of the Moon Ranch up this blue-ribbon trout stream. It was where we hosted opening-day-of-fishing-season parties, complete with erupting romances and disrupted marriages. Our house with weathered shakes and a screened porch is where the twins were conceived after one such party. In that narrow valley lit by sun in summer, dark in winter, drenched with moon any season, Eric and Steve chased grasshoppers for bait with their dad to catch the giant brown trout that fed in the creek. Our favorite fishing holes were lined with cottonwood trees and wound among pocket meadows where deer and bighorn sheep and the occasional moose or mountain lion came to drink.

The bungalow we rented had been built at the end of the nineteenth century as a fishing and hunting lodge by the Irish rancher who owned the Finlen Hotel in Butte. One wing was locked shut. We managed to breach the lock and found dusty zebra hides, mounted heads of water buffalo, elk and American bison, a moth-eaten bearskin rug, and African baskets. These were souvenirs of the big-game hunting businessmen and politicians who had gathered there as Finlen's guests—the most famous being Theodore Roosevelt. Too valuable to be left on walls for renters such as our family, the relic hides were disintegrating in the mouse-infested rooms where they'd been hidden away, and as far as I know are decaying there yet.

For me, Rock Creek is what Joan Didion in *The Year of Magical*

Thinking calls "a vortex." A place best avoided if you don't want to be submerged in nostalgia and melancholy. Vortex memory-pools like Rock Creek lie in wait at every watering hole from here to home. Take Clinton. In the eighties while Bill and I were returning from an arts conference in Helena, hatching the idea for what would become *The Last Best Place*, we saw a "rainbow at midnight" over the Clark's Fork River—an astounding silvery white arc backlit by a three-quarters moon.

A few years later, Bill and I were at the nearby Turah Pines Bar, where we had come to see Ernest Tubbs in one of his final appearances. Predictably, the last dance that night was "Rainbow at Midnight." I loved the song and memorized the words. "After the war was over / and I was coming back to you / I saw a rainbow at midnight / out on the ocean blue." I used them in my first published story, "It's Come to This." The story is about a ranch woman schoolteacher who loses her husband, takes up with a logger, and dances with a disfigured cowboy, which changes her life. It was chosen by Robert Stone to be included in the 1992 edition of *Best American Short Stories*.

End of the Road. At Bonner I exit the freeway and make the turn up Highway 200. I do not glance at the Milltown Bar—another vortex—for Dick Hugo is not on my mind, although a Beam ditch is. As we wind through the narrow canyon of the Big Blackfoot, the river riffles silver in moonlight—a lopsided moon above zigzag pines on the logged-off hillsides.

Bruno perks up, circles restless on his bed. I wonder if he recognizes the feel and flow of this familiar canyon passage. He moans softly, trying to tell me he wants out. I take a dog treat from its bag and hold it behind my head. I love the moist, gentle touch of Bruno's nose on my palm. I give him another treat.

"Almost there, baby boy."

Here at last is the turnoff to Bear Creek Road. My butt is so sore it's numb. My eyes are blurring. There is a dull pain in my right thigh. It is past nine in the evening and I've been pushing the pedal for more than twelve hours. I'm too old for this, I think. Never again!

About a mile and a half up the road, I pass a row of mailboxes, not stopping to open mine. We bump over the first cattle guard and tunnel through pines on both sides of the graveled track. Metal roofs gleam on new houses at the edge of the forest. The overgrazed pasture on our left has gone to dirt. We pass Trichel's deserted double-wide set up on blocks, and the forest closes in right up to my gate.

When I bump over my cattle guard the meadow opens to the light of the moon. Black white-faced Hereford cows and calves with new brands scabbed on their haunches clutter our rutted road. These belong to the Wills family, who have put their cows out on our pasture every Memorial Day since our first spring in 1971, when old Ernest and dark-haired young Sidney road horseback to the Little House to ask permission. Now Ernest is dead and Sidney has gotten wide in the belly and gimpy and gray like me, and can be as cranky as he is funny. I honk the horn. The animals scatter. I open the metal gate that leads to our driveway, shooing away a few insistent mamas and babies.

Our white-chinked log house is lit upstairs and down, looming in the new grass like a ship at sea. My ship. My sea.

"Brunie," I cry. "We're home!"

Leftovers. In the glare from my headlights I see Bill's sturdy shape. His large head with its thatch of white hair is thrust forward, and his shoulders are hunched as he hurries toward the driveway at the front of the house.

Brunie doesn't wait for me to let him out the back. He leaps over my seat, almost knocking Bill over. Bill grabs me in a bear hug.

"You made it!"

He kisses me hard on the mouth. I smell tobacco—the gin on his breath, a whiff of lime. Do I imagine the salt of dried tears?

"So glad you're back." Bill puts his arm across my shoulder, and bound tight, we walk around the house to the back deck. Bruno has been sniffing the yard, rediscovering territory. He beats me to Steve, jumps up onto his chest grunting in Bruno language.

"Hi there, buddy," says Steve. He pushes the dog down and comes to me. I hold my big boy. Steve is getting hefty with an incipient beer belly. Still, his face is unlined. His smile is pure welcome.

"Too late for the salmon," I say.

"Saved you a piece."

"Bruno's hungry. What I am is thirsty!"

Chris and Rhonda are sitting in my Target-special wooden chairs at the round slatted table on the deck. The table is cluttered with beer bottles and half-drunk gin and tonics. An ashtray is filled with the partly smoked butts of Bill's menthol extra lights. Chris is a large man, dark haired and heavyset, with a five-o'clock shadow. I see very little of his father in him. He stands up, almost formally, and holds out his hand. I give him a hug. He pulls away awkward because we're practically strangers and besides, Kittredges are not a huggy bunch (the opposite of Deutches). Bruno sits on Chris's foot, then rolls onto his back, legs up, begging a tummy rub. Chris laughs. There is nothing like a big goofy dog to break the ice.

"Got any more of that gin and tonic?" I say. I am introduced to Rhonda, a small, slender woman with outsized gray eyes that are slightly protruding. There are dark circles under the eyes tonight.

"They've had a tough day," says Bill. "Packed up Pat's stuff. It was hotter than hell in that apartment! I left them to it. All those boxes."

"We've thrown out a lot. Gave a bunch to the Salvation Army," says Rhonda.

Chris doesn't say much. He is a mechanical engineer working in Portland, a graduate of the Oregon Institute of Technology in his hometown of Klamath Falls. He says that competing with big-city grads from the university in Eugene is like being the outsider at a fraternity party. "They've pretty much got the good jobs sewed up. But we're doing all right."

Rhonda has worked for the FBI since graduating from high school. She resembles the television detective girls of *Without a Trace* or *Cold Case*, or Sergeant Barbara Havers in BBC's *Inspector Lynley Mysteries* series—diminutive and intense, with high cheekbones and straight brown hair. "I'm not an agent," she explains. "I just take care of the office."

I like Rhonda immediately. I'm sure she's adept at keeping secrets for the guys in suits and ties. She is Chris's second wife, a far cry from his blonde first spouse, rumored to be a drug-addicted motorcycle woman whom I never met but have heard about. Rhonda and Chris seem determined to make their family a secure haven. They have a child of their own and are taking care of Chris's two daughters.

Pat rarely talked about his family, but he asked me one winter what he should buy as a Christmas present for his littlest granddaughter in Portland. I was touched that he would come to me for advice. He showed me her picture. A cute little girl with blonde curls. I was surprised he carried that picture. Surprised he sent presents to anyone, although I shouldn't have been, for he was generous with us.

I remember the last Christmas we spent with Pat, him sitting in an old oak armchair in my living room across from Bill on the other side of the fireplace. Pat wore a red V-neck sweater; Bill's was maroon. My sons and their pretty wives swirled back and forth delivering presents from the great pile under our Christmas tree. (My father would have called such excess obscene.) The tree was a ceiling-high ponderosa cut from our woods and decked out with bird ornaments and winking lights.

Pat's gift to me was a set of white ceramic casseroles, and his gift to Bill was a two-volume set of *New Yorker* cartoons. He wanted us to cook and to laugh. We gave Pat *Karl Bodmer's America*—watercolors and drawings made in the 1830s of Hidatsa, Assiniboine, and Blackfeet Indians; of bison in the Missouri Breaks; and the river's haunting chalk cliffs described so vividly by Lewis and Clark. We wanted Pat to have something beautiful to hold in his hands after his all-night janitorial travails.

Pat's absence is palpable. I drink my gin and pick at the cold slab of salmon that Steve has brought me. The circle of people around this table—family, however distant—chats quietly and a bit awkwardly. After racing cross-country, the calm of this small gathering is a comedown. It seems there should be more drama. More grief. In many cultures, when a death in the family arrives, there will be wailing, ululation, fingers cut off at the joint, long braids sawed to the root. But for us, mourning is bound by the constraints of a puritanical code. No excess allowed.

People like us join with family and friends to feast on fish or ham or beans and rice around a circular table. Sorrow is the context and weeping is likely, but there will be no tearing of hair. We toast the dead with a glass of wine, a beer, a cup of sparkling water. And then, if you are at my house, we wash and dry the dishes.

Runaway Redux. Bruno is here. Bruno is gone. Oh my God, Brunie is gone! In the commotion of arriving and meeting and eating and drinking and saying goodbyes, I've lost track of my traveling companion. I search the cave-like TV room where Bruno likes to sleep on the battered couch. He is not on the dog bed in my upstairs bedroom. Not in his pen. I grab an oversized flashlight and look under the front steps where he likes to cool off. Finally, I check the woodshed where we found him asleep years ago when we thought we'd lost him his first night at the ranch.

I call for Bruno and call again. It is around midnight but I don't worry about waking my neighbors for I am out of their sight and beyond human earshot. My voice echoes back from the pine forest and fades away. I'm immersed in a silence, dark and tactile as black velvet. The moon has gone down and the night is heavy with stars. I see nothing beyond the glow of my porch light. I hear nothing but the yapping of a faraway dog. Not Bruno.

Bill has been preparing for bed. He puts his pants back on and begins calling, too. Still no answer, no movement, no dog. When our little foundling Red Dog disappeared, I tracked him. He never came back. I've called for lost cats: our calico Miss Tree killed by a coyote; and the pink-eared Itza kitten likely snatched by an owl; gray Gorky was shot by a neighbor; and we found my all-time favorite declawed dog-cat Rascal dead near the barn—a big sweet tiger who couldn't defend himself. This meadow is hell on cats, except for stay-at-homes like black-and-white Ceca, who ruled over our other cats and dogs and lived to age eighteen. Or shy black Kevin, who slept in the closet all day, hunted at night, and enjoyed being humped by species-confused Brunie.

I've waited for disappeared teenage sons to come home, too, calming myself, trying to be optimistic. They, however, could call me on the telephone. Or I could track them down through friends. I have dialed up emergency rooms, the police, and sheriff departments to no avail, hoping there'd been no accident and half-sure the bad boys would appear, as they always did, disheveled and hungover, cocky or apologetic. Boys could understand my panic, feel my fury, make up excuses and lies, but finally ask forgiveness in whatever backhanded way they contrived. Not so with animals whose lack of language makes them defenseless even at their most infuriating.

"He'll come back," says Bill. "Bruno always comes back. He's a male. He's out hunting females. Staking territory."

Bill is right. Bruno has grown up here. We've been gone only two weeks. He can't be lost. But there is nothing rational about how I feel. "Let's take the car and look for him. Now!"

Bill is so glad to have me home he will go on a wild dog chase in the middle of the night to please me. We drive across the cattle guard, across the meadow, and into the woods, taking the turn onto the west fork of Bear Creek Road and down toward Holbrook's bottomland. I stop every hundred yards, get out of the car, and call for Bruno. No sign of him—no barking except from a dog whose owner is probably getting out of bed and grabbing his shotgun. There is nothing to do but go home.

I slam the car door, take one look across my dim lawn, and make one last call. "Brunie, come!"

And here he is, casually trotting toward us from wherever he's been, head down, thick tail wagging from side to side. Bruno stops a few yards away, considering what to do next. His eyes, caught in the beams of our porch light, gleam yellow. He knows he's been a bad boy and so do I, but I can't bear punishing him tonight. I stoop to his height, clap my hands.

"Come, boy, come on. I've got a treat for you."

At the word "treat" Brunie marches straight to my feet. He sits like a good dog. I wrap my arms around his furry neck, damp with night dew. Bill laughs.

"Spoiled mutt. Told you he'd be back."

Bill takes my hand as we enter the house. Bruno dogs our steps. It's been a long, long day. Tomorrow is a smear of amber on the horizon. This journey is over. It is time to go to bed.

AFTER WORDS

My journey across the plains with Bruno was over, but journeys don't end, they merely stop for a while then continue down a different path or—more accurately—many paths. A couple of weeks after we returned home, my friends Susan and Roy O'Connor gave me a six-week-old black Lab who started me on a new trip. This pup was more finely wrought than Bruno—a sleek, inquisitive female with a pink tongue that loves to lick. We named her Lulu and thought she'd be the perfect mate for Bruno.

That was not to be. By the age of two, Lulu had been operated on twice to repair a leg joint that had no cartilage. She could run like a greyhound, but her injured leg could not take the weight of Bruno trying to mate. So we took her to be spayed and discovered she had the reproductive organs of a six-month-old pup and could never produce offspring. The dogs would have to be just pals, which they were until the sad winter solstice when Bruno died, too young at ten years.

Lulu and I have been inseparable ever since. Through the years, as I sit at my word processor, Lulu curls up at my feet and, precise as an alarm clock, starts nudging me in the late afternoon. She voices her signature roar and bounces up and down like a mechanical toy. It is time for our walk in the woods or across the meadow and along the creek—walks of a mile or two or three that have kept both of us fit into old age.

Now Lulu is twelve and I am seventy-nine, and who knows how many more walks either one of us has left. When her time comes—probably before mine—I will place Lulu's ashes next to Bruno's, which lie in a box alongside his collar and a clay mold of his great paw in a ceramic bowl made by my uncle Gene on a table built by Alex. The oversize table, crafted with slabs of wood from our barn, dominates the entrance to our living room. Above it on the log wall is a large bulletin board that Dave Smith put together in 1973, with photos of us in our thirties, portraits of Eric and Steve in sailor suits, Dick Hugo and Jim Crumley playing softball, and Jim Welch courting Lois at Rock Creek. There are photos of Alex and Andrew, newborns in Spain, and our Seattle friends on Pacific beaches or camping with us down in Hell's Canyon.

I have added letters of condolence from those same friends, sent after Dave died. And snapshots of our boys in their teens sporting hair to their shoulders, images of my mother and father, and a sympathy card featuring a grizzly bear waving his paw. The latest addition is a tribute to Bruno drawn in brown crayon with a big red heart by Elodie and Tilly, who rode him like a horse when they were toddlers and cuddled up to his furry belly.

The letters from friends, who in the meantime have also died, have faded. The photos are yellowing with edges curling, and the board is beginning to crumble. "It's too sad," says Alex, who faces the bulletin board while using his table as a desk. "It's ugly. You should put it upstairs in your bedroom."

"No," I say. I have no problem with death and decay. People and things crumble and dissolve while others rise fresh and green: wildflowers, new puppies, and grandkids. This forty-one-year-old bulletin board is our *memento mori*, dedicated to our family's history. It may not be beautiful, but "it's our shrine," says Steve. "I say it stays," says Eric. "Right," says Andrew. Bill nods from his armchair by the fireplace. Alex is outvoted.

As for Bruno's ashes, and Lulu's to come, we will bury them some spring (there is no hurry) on the little clay hill by the house where ponderosas have grown tall over forty years and the wild apple blooms, and where some of our cats are buried. We will mark the dogs' graves with stones or crosses and sing a dog song, maybe read a dog poem, but the ceremony will not be an extended ritual like the elaborate disposal of my mother's ashes.

Mom died of chronic pneumonia the day before her 101st birthday. Even then, she did not go easy. As she'd instructed, during our extended family's memorial celebration in June, we buried *some* of her ashes next to our father's on the dune in Sawyer overlooking Lake Michigan. Mom's second instruction had been "throw them in the lake." So we inflated a rubber raft and Kathy tumbled into it holding up her broken leg with its cast and clutching the box of ashes. Carole and I stepped warily into ice-cold waters. When our feet lost touch, we gasped and shivered, propelling the raft out past the sandbar into deep water. Then we began to giggle. "What are you two hooting about?" asked Kat. "Mom," said Carole between guffaws. "She's laughing her guts out." "Revenge," I snorted. "Testing us to the end."

But the main event happened the night before at a beach barbecue held by family and friends to celebrate Mom's life, when we shot two fireworks rockets loaded with handfuls of Mom's ashes toward the full moon. The rockets whistled as they climbed, exploded skyward trailing stars blue, green, and red, then plummeted into the lake. Mom applauded from wherever her spirit had flown.

"Say something in Hungarian," Andrew and Alex shouted. I blurted out *kezét csókolom* (I kiss your hand) and *szervusz* (hello/goodbye). Which is the perfect double-minded Hungarian greeting.

Szervusz is what I say to you readers. And *kezét csókolom* to the family and friends who have supported me through many versions of this book over ten years. Thanks go to my sons: Andrew and Alex, who read and critiqued early manuscripts. And to Eric and Steve for their stories. And to my sisters, Kathy Tatlock and Carole Deutch, for their memories—rarely the same as mine. More thanks to Carolyn Patterson, who helped me edit a near-final version. And to Seattle friends Anne Stadler and Lucy Dougall for comments in the "Lilacs" section. Thanks to Bill Kittredge, whose words and knowledge have helped me on the long road trip of becoming a writer. And thanks, finally, to Daniel Simon, copyeditor extraordinaire, to the exacting proofreader, Tanya Grove, and to Barbara Ras—my editor and publisher—who welcomed this odd story about a journey with a dog and recognized something of value in it. I kiss your hands, one and all.

ANNICK SMITH is a writer and filmmaker whose work focuses on the literature and history of the Northern Rockies. Her books include the memoir *Homestead*, the Montana anthology *The Last Best Place*, which she edited with William Kittredge, and *Big Bluestem*, about Oklahoma's tallgrass prairies. Her articles, essays, and stories have appeared in *Audubon*, *Outside*, *National Geographic Traveler*, the *New York Times*, and *Story* and have been widely anthologized. She was executive producer of the film *Heartland*, a co-producer of *A River Runs Through It*, and producer of the public television series *The Real People*, about Native Americans in the Inland Northwest. Smith is a founding board member of the Sundance Film Institute and founder of Hellgate Writers, a literary center in Missoula. She has lived in western Montana since 1964.